More Praise for *Make Talent Yc*

"In this much-needed book, Axelrod and Coyle present the first research-based analysis of *what successful talent developers actually do*! The reader is then provided with a framework including specific and highly learnable behaviors. The best part for me, the framework is based upon a fundamental truth: real development occurs *on the job* and needs to be an integral part of getting important work accomplished."

—**Edmund B. Piccolino, PhD, former head of human resources at PepsiCo International, EMI Music, and Kodak Polychrome Graphics and Managing Director, Piccolino Associates**

"As a senior leader striving for market-leading, game-changing results, I always knew that our people were the key differentiator. Wendy and Jeannie have uncovered the practical actions that allow managers to develop people and achieve superior business results!"

—**Amy S. Abrams, former Senior Vice President, Merck, and former President, Telerx**

"This is a must-read for any line manager and HR executive who 'gets it' and knows that development is what competitive organizations and employees crave. This book provides the art and the science of the what, the why, and the how."

—**Beverly Kaye, founder and CEO, Career Systems International, and coauthor of *Love 'Em or Lose 'Em***

"People are a company's most important asset. *Make Talent Your Business* provides a powerful set of practices that will help leaders drive development and empower their employees to succeed."

—**Ray Davis, President and CEO, Umpqua Bank, and author of *Leading for Growth***

"The perfect blend of compelling research, real-life scenarios, and tools for success. Wendy and Jeannie's insights remind us that developing people and getting results are not a trade off. Share this with anyone wanting to link talent to increased business results."

—**Mary Eckenrod, Vice President, Global Talent Management, Research In Motion (makers of the BlackBerry), and former Vice President, Worldwide Talent, Kraft Foods**

"Right on target! A very useful guide to talent management. Full of great tips and how-to-do-it advice."

—**Ed Lawler, Distinguished Research Professor of Business, Marshall School of Business, University of Southern California, and author of _Talent_**

"Talent development is a driving focus of excellent organizations. The authors make a compelling case that any leader can apply these practices. I intend to use this great template with my leaders to increase operating results and develop talent."

—**Cynthia Kiser Murphey, President and Chief Operating Officer, New York–New York Hotel and Casino**

"People are an organization's differentiator _and_ most valuable asset. This book pinpoints the practices of managers who successfully develop the leaders of the future."

—**Mike Panigel, Senior Vice President, Human Resources, Siemens Corporation**

"The old adage of 'teaching a man to fish' was never more apropos than in Wendy and Jeannie's expert road map. They provide a must-read for every manager to help talent flourish and in the process create an enduring managerial legacy."

—**Kevin Oakes, CEO, Institute for Corporate Productivity (i4cp), and coeditor of _Executive Guide to Integrated Talent Management_**

"Companies and managers still struggle to find effective approaches for developing leaders at every level who can outperform the competition. The authors have harvested their extensive experience and research to serve up this definitive guide for cultivating talent to achieve extraordinary business results."

—**Tom Kaney, former Senior Vice President, Human Resources, GlaxoSmithKline**

Make Talent Your Business

Make Talent Your Business

*How Exceptional Managers Develop
People While Getting Results*

Wendy Axelrod & Jeannie Coyle

Berrett–Koehler Publishers, Inc.
San Francisco
a BK Business book

©2011 by Wendy Axelrod and Jeannie Coyle

All rights reserved. No part of this publication may be reproduced, distributed, or transmitted in any form or by any means, including photocopying, recording, or other electronic or mechanical methods, without the prior written permission of the publisher, except in the case of brief quotations embodied in critical reviews and certain other noncommercial uses permitted by copyright law. For permission requests, write to the publisher, addressed "Attention: Permissions Coordinator," at the address below.

Berrett-Koehler Publishers, Inc.
235 Montgomery Street, Suite 650
San Francisco, CA 94104-2916
Tel: (415) 288-0260   Fax: (415) 362-2512   www.bkconnection.com

Ordering Information
Quantity sales. Special discounts are available on quantity purchases by corporations, associations, and others. For details, contact the "Special Sales Department" at the Berrett-Koehler address above.

Individual sales. Berrett-Koehler publications are available through most bookstores. They can also be ordered directly from Berrett-Koehler: Tel: (800) 929-2929; Fax: (802) 864-7626; www.bkconnection.com

Orders for college textbook/course adoption use. Please contact Berrett-Koehler: Tel: (800) 929-2929; Fax: (802) 864-7626.

Orders by U.S. trade bookstores and wholesalers. Please contact Ingram Publisher Services, Tel: (800) 509-4887; Fax: (800) 838-1149; E-mail: customer.service@ingrampublisherservices. com; or visit www.ingrampublisherservices.com/Ordering for details about electronic ordering.

Berrett-Koehler and the BK logo are registered trademarks of Berrett-Koehler Publishers, Inc.

Printed in the United States of America.

Berrett-Koehler books are printed on long-lasting acid-free paper. When it is available, we choose paper that has been manufactured by environmentally responsible processes. These may include using trees grown in sustainable forests, incorporating recycled paper, minimizing chlorine in bleaching, or recycling the energy produced at the paper mill.

Library of Congress Cataloging-in-Publication Data

Axelrod, Wendy.
    Make talent your business: how exceptional managers develop people while getting results /
    Wendy Axelrod & Jeannie Coyle. -- 1st ed.
       p. cm.
    Includes bibliographical references and index.
    ISBN 978-1-60509-931-6 (pbk. : alk. paper)
    1. Supervision of employees. 2. Personnel management. 3. Performance. 4.
    Employees--Training of. 5. Career development. I. Coyle, Jeannie. II. Title.
    HF5549.12.A94 2011
    658.3--dc22   2011010367

First Edition
16 15 14 13 12 11   10 9 8 7 6 5 4 3 2 1

Interior design and project management by Jonathan Peck, Dovetail Publishing Services.
Cover design: Marquardt Art/Design
Cover photo: © Mikael Damkier/Alamy

We dedicate this book, with love, to those who have most inspired and spurred us to grow more every day—Jacob Johanson, Aaron Johanson, Andrew Johanson, and Jim Coyle, and to those wonderfully devoted managers who on a day-to-day basis develop people as they get results. They light a path not often taken.

Contents

Foreword

Dave Ulrich

DURING A RECENT INTERVIEW, an executive with a large investment firm asked me if the principles regarding talent and people my firm advocated would cause his people to work harder for the same money, so that he could buy a bigger yacht. I was stupefied and not sure how to respond. I realized that leadership Neanderthals continue to exist who worship the escapades of Gordon Gekko, the hero of the *Wall Street* movies.

Fortunately, fewer and fewer leaders practice traditional command-and-control, greed-is-good, self-interest-rules leadership. More leaders recognize the importance of communicating and coaching, generosity over greed, and service to others more than self-interest. These enlightened leaders understand that business is about people, inside the company and as investors and customers outside the company. Simply stated, when people are at the heart of business, business operates better.

But while pledging that "people are our most important asset" is easy to say, it is not always easy to do. Wendy Axelrod and Jeannie Coyle insightfully, wisely, and clearly close the knowing-versus-doing gap. They are uniquely qualified to help modern

---

Dave Ulrich is a business professor at the University of Michigan, a partner in the RBL Consulting Group, winner of the Nobels Colloquia Prize for Leadership on Business and Economic Thinking, and the best-selling author of two dozen books on business leadership.

leaders become exceptional development managers (EDMs) who create exceptional developing employees (EDEs). They have combined decades of personal experience in identifying and developing leaders, they are informed consumers of theory and research, and they have thoughtfully interviewed EDMs and EDEs to find out how to "make talent your business." I have known them for many years and knew of their passion for developing people while getting results. What I learned by reading their book was how clearly and cleverly they can turn complex ideas into doable actions. Their book shares stories of real managers who have learned how to develop people and then translates these cases into practical principles.

The result of their experience and work are five practices that will help any manager turn the rhetoric of talent management into the reality of competent and committed people.

As I savored their insights, I was reminded of a set of Russian matryoshka (nesting) dolls, in which the doll hidden inside each larger doll shows increasing detail and craftsmanship. The five practices Wendy and Jeannie propose are only the outer image of the further refinements they offer for helping leaders better develop and manage their people. As a result, their book became increasingly richer and more fulfilling the more I delved into each chapter. Leaders who understand the principles and access the practices the authors offer will recognize the pathway to becoming an EDM.

Managers who make every day a development day will discover that development is not a sidebar to work but work itself. Our research has revealed that top companies for leadership had managers who spent about 25 to 30 percent of their time on developing future leaders. Sometimes when we present this finding, leaders gawk and wonder how that is possible with the press of business. Wendy and Jeannie offer very concrete examples of how leaders develop others every day and every way.

When managers tap into the psychological side of development, not only do they look in the personal mirror that reflects their own behavior, but they also try to understand why employees do what they do. We have found in our research that when employees have a *why* to work, the *what* and the *how* of work are much easier to accomplish.

Leading others is a team sport as evidenced in the principle of connecting people with development partners. Partners may be friends, colleagues, or social media associates. These partners offer support and build peer pressure to help people develop.

Organizations don't think; people do—and when people think and act, there are inevitably political and relationship overtones. Managers who develop people master the practice and teach skills to navigate the political terrain. As managers help others recognize and engage in the positive aspects of political discourse, they help people learn to make things happen.

Finally, managers who develop people shape their environment to drive development. We have found in our work that when leaders are meaning makers, employees are not only competent and committed but also fully contributing with their heart and soul. Creating an organization where this sense of purpose is abundantly instilled in all employees becomes a primary leadership agenda.

As each of these five practices is assessed and accessed, leaders can become development managers. What is particularly impactful is how these five practices overlap and build on each other. The truly exceptional leaders of the future will not only understand but put these practices into action.

Of course, like the tradition-bound leader who interviewed me and was more concerned about self-interest than service to others, not all leaders will be able to lead the employees of the future. But with help from outstanding books like this one, leaders who want to lead exceptional employees will be more able to do so. And leaders who rely on historically autocratic approaches to leadership will find themselves increasingly isolated from both people who care and from business results that matter.

Thanks, Wendy and Jeannie, for this marvelous treatise and guide on becoming exceptional development managers.

Introduction

Helping Good People Get Better Every Day

WOULDN'T IT BE HEAVENLY if the people you manage were developing new skills while they delivered results every day? They would be more productive, happier, *and* less likely to leave. You'd get a kick out of seeing their personal and professional growth and building the "human assets" of not only your department but also your company.

Pipedream or possibility within reach? Our research demonstrates that there are exceptional managers who make this dream a reality every single day. They are masters at making talent their business—a business they get down to every day while achieving good and often great results. You, too, can grow talent while you grow results by learning and applying the five powerful practices these exceptional managers use. Through extensive research into their development tactics, we have distilled their success into actionable, practical advice you can adopt starting now—even though you're already feeling busy and overwhelmed. In this book, we share stories of managers just like you who have made the switch and seen their people, their results, and their own careers soar.

A manager we'll call Lori certainly made it happen in her team. Let's start with her story.

1

A Manager Who Grows People Like Crazy

"Developing talented people is an imperative for me," says Lori. "If I don't, good people leave. It's my job to make their work a bit 'edgy' for them. That way, they are always learning." She assembles and manages teams of people assigned to high-impact projects. She could simply hire fully experienced people, leave them to it, and then step in to help if they hit a roadblock, but that's not how Lori manages.

Instead, Lori deliberately staffs the teams to create huge opportunities for development—development that supports the job at hand as well as skill development that deepens and broadens her employees' abilities. Like a master chef, she likes to go beyond predictable meat and potatoes. She mixes things up by bringing together all kinds of people with varying tastes and talents and deftly combines them into a "gourmet" type of team. An expert in unusual combinations, she layers newbies with tenured folks. In her teams, you are likely to find people who possess great client interface skills mixed with those who are technically competent but not so good with clients, and so forth. As people implement the project work, they can turn to each other for support to address their skill gaps.

Lori takes risks with people by giving them both the latitude and the explicit *requirement* to learn. Somehow, she's figured out how to put together these unconventional "entrees" without risking project results. An appreciative member of her staff describes her secret sauce as "intertwining performance and development . . . with performance taking priority."

When we asked the people Lori manages how they feel about being pushed out of their comfort zone to learn more, we heard time and time again answers like, "She pushed me." We learned that Lori is very skilled at getting to know each person and developing trust and rapport. Once Lori had a solid understanding of each of her employees, she was in a good place to know just how far to push them. They then trust that she won't let them get in a career-limiting accident. Because of the high trust, they also open their minds and hearts to the direct and sometimes tough feedback Lori gives them to support their growth. One person applauds Lori's unusual, honest, and candid approach as "nonhierarchical" (not like the boss talking down to me) and more conversational. With this approach, her delivery of hard-hitting feedback works. Instead of engaging in "hit and run" feedback, Lori initiates an ongoing discussion in which she shares her experiences and provides the context for action.

Lori is also very clever at setting up "development partners" for her fast-learning staff. It's not that she doesn't teach her staff herself—she does. But she also sees the value in helping each of her employees configure a network of people who can teach them expansive and deeper skills beyond what they need to know to perform today's tasks. One of her staff said, "She encouraged me to network and build developmental relationships and opened my eyes to the importance of exposure to other people as a key to my development. It was a way to stretch my thinking and skills."

Lori creatively infuses the environment with learning—not just classroom training programs but simple things and abiding attention. Her brown-bag learning lunches, spirited brainstorming sessions, and learning circles remind us of college study groups. They feature important learning in bite-size pieces close to the action. All these approaches together have a way of naturally sending a signal about the importance of development. While many managers pay lip service to it being OK to learn from failure, Lori truly does create a work environment in which people will take some risks to try new things. When people fail, she promptly provides empathy and feedback and then quickly turns the discussion to lessons learned.

By now you're probably thinking Lori is working overtime to do all this. We assure you that she is neither burning the midnight oil nor feeling overworked. Lori is actually working less because her staff's growing capability means they get better results faster than simply focusing on near-term performance. And she's doing less cleanup of mistakes made by her people. Less time, less frustration, more productivity—sounding pretty good, isn't it?

It gets better. Although Lori says she uses this approach because she would lose people if she didn't, she also says she reaps many more benefits than low staff turnover. She's also told us she's growing her *own* skills. She shared that she takes great joy and pride in what she is doing, so much so that what she brings home to share with her husband are almost all stories about growing people—not just stories about growing results. We also happen to know that she's a downright talent magnet. Her reputation draws good people to her, and she therefore gets to pick from the best. We suspect senior management notices her great people development and business results, and we predict she'll be promoted because of them. Her "graduates" tell us that they're applying what they learned from Lori as they manage others, a great example of "paying it forward" to magnify the people development effect.

Embedded in Lori's management style are the five powerful practices that we discovered when we did our research on exceptional managers who are great at developing people. These are managers who, like Lori, reach well beyond getting performance from people to also developing their deeper and broader skills every day. We're talking about skills that allow employees to extend and add to their reach—such as influencing people to accept changes, taking the lead in projects, identifying breakthroughs to products and processes. After sharing just a bit about our research, we'll call out the five practices that form the core of this book.

Identifying and Closing the Talent Development Gap

We are both passionate about talent development, and a central theme of our careers has been advancing development from many avenues. Jeannie has been a senior vice-president of human resources at American Express, building the company's first extensive talent development system. Wendy directed a *Fortune 50* company's corporate university and talent management function. She also started up a highly successful mentoring program for professionals in the greater Philadelphia area. We have similar consulting and coaching practices and share a deep and abiding passion about the overriding significance of the manager in developing the potential of people. Together, we have over fifty years of experience in organizational development, talent management, leadership development, succession planning, and executive coaching in over one hundred organizations, from start-ups to *Fortune 100*s, in a wide variety of industries, including financial services, pharma, health care, high tech, manufacturing, telecom, and education. We're proud of the fact that we spent decades of our careers in organizations, learning about them from the inside, before going out to start our practices. We've taught literally thousands of managers to coach and develop people, both in workshops and as part of our executive coaching practices.

In the course of our varied careers, we have seen and read much that has made us determined to help identify and close the gap between the promise of developing people's potential and the stark reality that the promise is not fulfilled. For example, a few years ago, a highly reputable firm specializing in leadership development reported on the most and least used of the 67 behaviors (not 5, not 50, and not 100, but exactly 67) proven to make up good leadership. At the time, the company already had an enormous database that included over 10,000 rated leaders in 160 top companies. Out of the 67 behaviors tracked, "developing others" consistently came out near the bottom in terms of leadership behaviors actually used on the job.[1] Keep in mind that the sample included many leaders from companies that produced good results. You would expect that these subjects were likely to be managers with some training and the expectation that they develop their people.

So how could this be? Companies say they want managers to develop people. They tell their stakeholders so most convincingly and laud "developing people" as a top priority in their annual reports. They invest millions in leadership coaching and training. They use 360-degree feedback instruments galore. They renovate performance management processes, including development planning approaches, again and again. If we are to believe the data—and we do because it reflects much of our experience in organizations—in spite of all this corporate effort, managers are spending a very limited amount of their time developing staff. And there are doubts in some companies that even the time they spend is yielding good results. Managers float in a veritable sea of talent management tools and processes, but like the ancient mariner, many managers feel there is "Water, water everywhere but not a drop to drink."[2] To managers focusing on near-term results, these invented-elsewhere tools seem like a distraction rather than a lifeline.

We dug into the many credible studies that show that sufficient progress has not been made in finding effective ways to develop talent. For example, a 2008 Human Capital Institute study sponsored by Hewitt Associates revealed that while most organizations hold their executives and managers accountable for achieving business results, few hold managers (7 percent) or executives (10 percent) accountable for *developing* direct reports. Worse, only 5 percent of organizations say their managers consistently demonstrate the ability to develop their employees. The study concluded that these organizations were underinvesting in creating manager development capabilities.[3] McKinsey's ten-year follow-up to the "War for Talent" study echoes this same theme. It indicates that the talent shortage remains acute and has gotten worse.[4] McKinsey notes that the heavy investments made to date in talent management processes have proved to be "insufficient, superficial and wasteful."

Cynics in the field have said, "Managers will never develop people well enough. Just give up. Talent development is HR's job to do." We disagree. While we may be accused of being eternal optimists, we refuse to be grumpy pessimists. We believe there is hope, and it's in plain sight. The hope is you and thousands of other managers with unique day-to-day access and personal—and therefore intrinsically powerful—points of leverage. You are right in the heart of the most powerful environment for staff development. And we think you have a good sense of just how much you have to offer.

We were bolstered in this belief by working with some managers we met at a large insurance company. They longed to develop people but felt their desire exceeded their reach. In many ways, they expressed this desire to do more than simply helping employees do their "day jobs" well. Although many of these managers were accomplished people developers, they had a sense of being restricted by the pressure to "make the numbers." These managers told us they felt disconnected from the company's talent management processes and explained that they lacked the corporate support to significantly develop their people. With these frustrated but hopeful managers, we shared the old proverb, "Doubt is the beginning, not the end, of wisdom."

So if your intuition tells you that as a manager you have more to offer in meeting the need for developing talent, we agree. If your gut also tells you that you don't have all the answers for how to be great at developing people, know you are not alone. There are managers in all kinds of organizations with all the right intentions but few of the right skills or tangible support mechanisms to develop staff fully. Clearly, desire *and* doubt abound.

We knew there was a better answer for talent development, and we couldn't find it in the research. So we embarked on our own research to find the answer. We wanted to see when and *how* managers like you can make a big impact on developing talent. Our aim was—and is—to give motivated but perhaps doubtful managers the tools to develop the insights, skills, and a personal practice set to develop their people. Imprinted on our brains are the words of our colleague, Cal Wick, who has made learning the cornerstone of his career: "Learning cannot survive in a bell jar. It needs the support and immediacy of everyday application or it quickly suffocates."[5] We were determined to help you take learning out of the bell jar and bring it to life every day.

"About the Research," at the back of this book, provides details about our research methodology and results. We conducted in-depth interviews with more than seventy-five people in well-known companies such as Adidas, Booz Allen Hamilton, Corning, GE Interlogix, Genentech, GlaxoSmithKline, IBM, Intel, JPMorgan Chase, Kaiser Permanente, Kraft, L'Oréal, Marriott, Merck, Microsoft, Siemens, Wells Fargo, Wyeth, and Xerox, as well as smaller firms (twenty-eight companies in total). We spoke with both "exceptional development managers" (EDMs), whom we prequalified as people who truly develop the capacity of their employees beyond day-to-day performance needs, and "exceptional developing employees" (EDEs) who search out and seize growth opportunities. These EDMs and EDEs gave us countless hours of their time and a window into the story behind the story often told about how managers develop their people.

What we found from our research was eye-opening. We were able to distill a combination of insightful yet very practical approaches that have an incredible impact on developing people. The EDMs operate in a zone above and beyond the foundational management skills of delegating work, holding people accountable, and providing performance coaching and feedback. They do more than turn in expected business results and close skill gaps to get near-term results. They help people develop expanded and new skills for the future by generating *broad* and *deep* development—the very thing that most people hunger for and the EDEs we talked to demand.

The key finding is that EDMs embrace both development and results simultaneously, every day, in a way that makes the work itself powerfully developmental. In addition, we discovered four other practices that most or all EDMs use *in combination*. By melding the five practices, they make developing people notably more engaging, more time efficient, and more cost-effective. That's why they can do it without burning out their spirits, their energy, or their budgets.

They find that there are triple, even quadruple benefits to applying this unique combination of developmental practices. First and foremost, they grow the skills and value of individuals *while also* achieving superior business results. They take employees out of the territory of good day-to-day performance and help put them into a more mindful, customer-focused, organizationally sensitive zone and more able to manage complex work situations. In other words, they go beyond basic, near-term performance coaching to more expansive development coaching. In so doing, they recognize that they are investing the company's future talent—or, as the CEO or CFO might say, appreciating the company's human assets. EDMs also reap *personal* benefits, as they are also investing in themselves. They report greater job satisfaction because they escape the crossfire of daily pressures, and they have good reason to believe they are enhancing their reputations as valuable managers.

Do these managers conduct a daily cost-benefit analysis of developing staff? No; they feel no such need to calculate or communicate the specific value of what they're doing. While these managers are *our* heroes, they in no way consider themselves heroic. They are just doing their jobs as they see them. The difference is that for them, their job is making the numbers *and* developing people for the future. They find great satisfaction in what they do. Not one used the fancy word "steward" to describe himself or herself, but that is indeed what EDMs are: stewards of talent, managers who help good people get better every day.

This book brings their practices to life for you so that you can apply them in your organization. There's one chapter for each of the five practices embraced by the EDMs we studied. While much of what they do can take time to learn, most managers can implement these practices without complete support from the organization. Each chapter gives you real-life examples gathered in our research or experience within companies, good ideas to get you started, a tiny bit of development theory, and a just-in-time refresher course on some specific skills you'll need to put the concepts into action.

Chapter 6 encourages you to put your own EDM practices into action. We show you how to amplify your progress in learning these approaches, combine and sequence the individual practices, and anticipate the many rewards that accrue to you, your staff, and the organization. EDMs we spoke to didn't say they were into developing others for their own personal gain. Yet the truth is that you will increase your job satisfaction, reputation, and prospects by applying these practices for the benefit of others and your company. The conclusion of Chapter 6, focusing on the myriad of personal benefits you'll gain by becoming an EDM, is uplifting. Above all, you'll experience the gift of joy and pride that stems from making a real difference in people's lives and creating a legacy.

That difference can be as significant as opening a new frontier of possibility for your employees. This book's cover is a symbol of this transition. Imagine the smaller fish bowl as "today's work reality." When a manager provides basic performance coaching for an employee, it's like the fish, swimming more effectively in the smaller bowl. A good thing to do, no doubt. But by engaging in the five practices described in this book, an exceptional development manager makes expanded space available through stretch experiences *and* provides the foundation of support to encourage the person to make the initial, often scary jump to the bigger space. Once in the "bigger bowl," an employee has the opportunity to develop greater skills—and have a better time. The manager's developmental work simultaneously takes on a whole new dimension beyond performance coaching. It becomes a new blend of management work that is deliberate, resourceful, and continuous. Life in the bigger bowl is simply better for both employees and their managers. Once comfortable there, a still bigger bowl will call to them both. And so deep, continuous development becomes the new norm.

Your investment in the deep development of your people every day is a gift that opens door after door for them and for you. Your employees will experience the gift of opportunity and support to grow substantially at work. Your company will benefit from the gift of good employees who get better every day and who are motivated to stay and keep contributing themselves. In giving these gifts, you will have made talent your business and built a personal legacy.

This book provides you with the road map for making that transition. It's designed to show you how to act like the exceptional managers we studied. Developing talent in this way doesn't take extra budget for training or fancy processes or extra add-ons outside of work. It simply takes the creativity and diligence to use work as the main source of learning. EDMs learned what to do from experience. You get a head start by learning from them. The experience is there for the taking.

The Five Practices for Making Talent Your Business

Here are the five practices we discovered through our research with exceptional development managers and exceptional developing employees. The first one, "Make every day a development day," and the second one, "Tap the psychological side of development," are foundational. The others build on that base. Each of the practices can be used in the crevices of day-to-day work.

Using all five together works like a dream. For little investments of time, these managers reaped huge benefits in the growth of their people. We believe you can do the same.

1. Make Every Day a Development Day

EDMs demonstrate a way to go well beyond near-term performance to drive substantial development of people in order to ensure the organization's future growth. These managers use the work itself as the starting place to develop people. They add to and reshape work, stretching the space for people to grow skills *while* they are achieving expected "business" results. The EDMs are there every day as active participants and positive forces to support development on the job.

This practice is about adjusting your mind-set to focus on results and development simultaneously using "stretchy" work that develops people. It's a "two for one" approach that can be integrated into your day-to-day management. You'll find that this practice actually takes just a little time in the short term yet yields great performance and timesaving dividends over the long term as people become more skilled and more independent.

2. Tap the Psychological Side of Development

EDMs know that the effort they devote to developing people cannot be summarized into a step 1, step 2, step 3 approach, like you see in the directions for an IKEA furniture kit. Instead, the deep development employees seek involves learning complex skills like in-the-moment judgment, customer interface, and collaborative decision making. It turns out making an impact at that level necessitates development that's not just logical but also psychological.

Tapping into the psychological side of development involves creating a trusting relationship that makes it safe for your employees to open up to you, hear and act on your feedback, step out of their comfort zone, take risks, and become aware of their internal drivers. With all this new learning, employees find themselves much better equipped to handle their interactions. Getting to know them on a deeper level also helps you know just how far you can stretch them without going too far.

3. Connect People with Development Partners

You don't have to do all the development yourself. In fact, you shouldn't do it all. Take a page from EDMs who find ways to link with a number of other people as development partners for their employees. Spending the small amount of time it takes to connect people with others who have specific skills or experiences puts you in the enviable spot of sharing the development load. You open the door to expertise that goes beyond your own limitations while also increasing your staff's ability to find and work with other learning resources.

You start the process by helping your employees adjust any negative assumptions about reaching out to others. You then set the expectation and teach them how to make the most of these partner relationships. Importantly, you don't let go of the wheel once the match is made. Instead, you stay in touch to leverage lessons learned, look for gaps, and help fine-tune how people apply what they have learned.

4. Teach Skills to Navigate Organization Politics

Functional and technical skills can get your people only so far. To succeed, they also need to know how to navigate the politics of your organization and work appropriately to influence others. This isn't about cheating or manipulating the system. Rather, it is about being realistic and strategic regarding how decisions are made and having influence to make sure their ideas get heard.

EDMs help people map the political terrain, put together a plan of approach, and then learn and practice the skills to thrive in the terrain. This practice yields handsome benefits. Your people's efforts will be more efficient and effective. They end up producing results that really stick with those on the receiving end. Teaching these skills also reduces the time you spend cleaning up after political missteps.

5. Shape Your Environment to Drive Development

EDMs weave development into the very texture of their organizations, big or small. To do so, they add development abundance to their environment. They develop talent across the board—not just among a few high potentials—and circulate work challenges among team members to keep everyone on the learning edge.

Within their department, they make development an everyday expectation and hold people *and* themselves accountable for following through on development. They set the standard that learning is not an option but a requirement.

EDMs manage the interface between their world and the rest of the organization. They divert distractions from day-to-day development and ingeniously adapt talent development tools provided by the organization to their own needs. The result? An oasis of daily development that becomes not only a magnet for talent but also a prototype for the whole organization.

chapter 1 *Make Every Day a Development Day*

WHEN WE SUGGESTED TO JOE that he make every day a development day for his staff, he just about jumped out of his chair. "I've been trying to get two people to a required training course for the last five weeks and just can't work out the schedule. I am up to my eyeballs in projects and paperwork. How can I possibly make every day a development day? Sorry, but that's just nuts!"

You can probably relate to this harried manager. Good managers know how important it is to develop their people, but actually finding the time to do so is a challenge for them. Let's face it, it's a challenge for anyone in business these days. Fortunately, there are ways to go beyond what Joe saw as "nuts" (as in crazy) to nuts-and-bolts actions that make daily development a reality. Exceptional development managers (EDMs) we interviewed told us they use a dual approach to deliver a daily dose of development:

1. Deliberately building stretch into the work people do every day

2. Using their daily interactions with people to support that stretch

Surveyed EDMs overwhelmingly supported this winning combination. In fact, it was at the very top of their list of practices they value and actually put to use. What's more is that the exceptional developing employees (EDEs) we interviewed (the people who have done particularly well at developing in their careers) also ranked this kind of daily focus on development at the top of their list. That's why this practice is one of the two foundational elements for developing employees (the other is to tap the psychological side of development, which will be discussed in Chapter 2).

How to Make Every Day a Development Day

Imagine for a moment that you were asked to make every day at work a fitness day. Your first reaction might be to schedule time to go to the gym or to take the stairs instead of the elevator. But here's the hard part: you must stay in your very small office. Oh, and you have no budget to buy any fitness equipment—no treadmill, no elliptical trainer, not even weights. Give up? Anti-apartheid activist Nelson Mandela didn't. Confined to a small cell on Robben Island for the first eighteen of his twenty-seven years of incarceration, he found a way to make every day a fitness day. Keeping his long-term goal of being strong enough to lead the country beyond apartheid, he used whatever tools he had at hand—mainly his own body—to do calisthenics and make fitness part of his daily routine.[1]

Like Mandela, exceptional development managers use what is in front of them—namely, the work itself and their daily access to people doing it—to make bite-size progress on a big goal: continual development of the capacity of all their people so that they make talent their business.

If you were to observe these managers, you'd see two major trends. First, EDMs plan "stretch" into the work so that their people are continually pushing the boundaries of what they know and are comfortable doing. These managers are motivated to spend the little bit of extra time it takes to plan and support stretch because they know that the work at hand is the most powerful source of development. As one manager put it succinctly, "The work itself is the development. Experience is far and away the best teacher." We agree.

The second trend you'd spot is the way that exceptional managers spend their day. Instead of waiting to make a big (but infrequent) investment in development, they make lots of small (but frequent) deposits in their development account—think recurring short interactions versus infrequent formal meetings. They do this to help their people learn while doing work that stretches them. Another EDM we interviewed summed up this trend beautifully: "I approach development as an everyday 'being there' sort of thing, not as a programmatic process. I gently push people to do more than they think they can do. Then, if I see something, I note it and simply say it. I don't wait for a meeting or call it out as a developmental conversation."

Using the work itself as a major source of development is not a novel idea. The uncontested results of multiple research projects, some dating back to the 1980s, show that the vast majority of development comes from experience on the job, not from formal training programs.[2] Leadership guru Warren Bennis puts it this way: "I would argue that more leaders have been made by accident, circumstance, sheer grit, or will than have been made by all the leadership courses put together."[3] Yet according to research that mirrors our experience, fewer than one manager in ten uses the work at hand as a development tool.[4] Training is an important part of the mix, but too many managers still see sending people to programs as the panacea for development. When they do this, it lets them off the development hook, and that's unfortunate.

Are we saying that the one thing that matters most is done the least? Yes. We believe that a major reason that using the work itself as a development tool is so rare is that managers simply don't know how to package together work and development or how to put themselves in the picture every day to support development. The solution comes down to these four approaches that you can use to make every day a development day:

1. Tuck development into work
2. Create the right stretch
3. Seize development moments
4. Leverage team learning

1. Tuck Development into Work

EDMs are experts at creating development "twofers." You know the system: the hotel room that accompanies the plane ticket, the bottle of champagne that complements the purchase of a three-course meal. Marketers love to give attractive two-for-one deals—and we all love receiving them. EDMs achieve twofers by planning and shaping work so that employees go after one goal (business results) and along the way meet another one (development milestones). Here's how the twofer concept worked for an EDM we'll call Tim:

Tim was a sales and marketing manager for a small software company. He was committed to developing Gloria, a late-

twenties marketing manager who had just knocked his socks off by finishing a focus group project ahead of time while achieving great results AND teaching some interns how to properly conduct a focus group. She was chomping at the bit to learn more. Tim assigned her to lead a large and exciting project to design a new market approach for India. The market launch was a mere six months away. Gloria's team included financial analysts, HR specialists, and a consultant expert in doing business in India. Tucked into this assignment was lots of potential learning: about the Indian market, about creating a business plan that included financial analysis, and about getting the most from an expert consultant without letting him hijack the project. Tim took the time to talk Gloria through the assignment up front, making sure she knew there was a double finish line. He told her, "There are two ribbons waiting for you at the finish line: a results ribbon and a development ribbon." Then he went on to very specifically describe the expected results and what he wanted Gloria to learn while achieving these results.

What Tim and other exceptional managers do is not only tuck development into daily work but also create a simple, very strong combo development-and-performance plan. Tim didn't just tack a development plan onto Gloria's performance objectives, as routine performance management processes often suggest. Instead, he used one recurring planning process that put development right in the middle, on the way to results, so to speak, not at the end.

Imagine yourself giving people goals that will stretch them while they achieve important results. Be inspired by an EDM we know who said, "If you build developmental goals in, you improve the chances that they will be achieved. The results are better too, because the learning fuels higher levels of performance. So if someone has a goal to 'improve communication' in an execution plan, the person will not view development as extra stuff. You send a strong message—grow and learn while you are at work."

 Good Ideas . . .
For Tucking Development into Work

OK, so maybe you're not in charge of opening new markets around the world. How can you tuck development into the work you do manage? The opportunities are endless. Start by considering these:

» New demands on your department that you can turn into skill-building work that will stretch your employees

» Tasks on your plate that are routine for you but would be good learning opportunities for others

» Opportunities for people to reshape their work to include tasks that are developmentally rich from their point of view

» People who hold critical knowledge and can be tapped to transfer knowledge to colleagues

» Communications that provide individuals with a stronger line of sight to business strategy in order to pep up and enrich their day-to-day tasks

Another approach is to encourage someone to take a side trip from a core job to pick up something he or she can bring back and apply. Imagine a football player taking a ballet class as part of his practice regimen. Before you get too distracted by visions of a hefty running back up on tippy toes, think about the potential of this kind of cross-training. Some NFL stars do, in fact, take ballet because it teaches them physical lessons about balance and nimbleness that improve their moves on the field. Here are some "off-road" experiences from the world of work:

> *Gregg, a supervisor in the Auto Maintenance Pool, was known for his rough feedback style. He had a habit of losing good employees. His boss, Walt, decided to have him spend time working on the customer response line handling customer complaints. With this experience, which began with a short training course, Gregg learned some new communication skills such as how to be responsive to irate customers and leave each with a positive impression instead of a negative one.*
>
> *Sydney was a staff project manager who used the same planning method over and over and expected everyone to comply with her way of doing things. Spencer, her manager, wanted her to vary her style. He assigned her to the corporate advertising department with the specific charge to learn how the same communication challenge could be addressed from four or five different angles using six different channels.*

Once you have pinpointed what development you want people to acquire in a side trip, you'll need to engage them in actually taking the side trip and acquiring the learning that fits their development goals. It's important to take each of the four steps. To illustrate these steps, let's pick up the story of Gregg, the supervisor of the Auto Maintenance Pool. Gregg will be taking a learning side trip to customer service. See what his manager, Walt, told him in each of the key steps.

Get the person to recognize that the skill to be developed will make him more successful in his job.

> "Gregg, you're very direct with people. As we discussed before, the way you talk sometimes turns people off. It's as if you have one tool in your toolbox but you could use a few more. How about exploring other ways to influence people—ways that will work on your job and help you retain good people?"

Sell the particular development idea as a fast and effective way to learn and practice new skills.

> "There's nothing like going to a new place to learn something. Gregg, have you ever been on vacation and picked up a new way to fish or learned how to scuba dive? Going to customer service where people deal with confused or angry customers is a great place to find out different ways to deal with people. You'll get a chance to develop a new tool and try something new away from your current job and staff."

Express your support and respond to the person's concerns and needs.

> "I know that this new role will feel strange. Learning new skills always does. What concerns do you have about making this side trip into customer service, and how can I help?"

Engage the person in coming up with solutions.

> "Gregg, I know you are concerned about what your staff will think of your involvement with customer service. Some of them might get nervous about a change in your role or that you might not be available to them when they need you. Let's first figure out a time schedule for you with customer service that you can live with and then craft a conversation you can have with your team."

2. Create the Right Stretch

A challenge of tucking development into work is to plan just the right amount of stretch that builds skills without pushing people too far beyond their limits. Let's look at some ways that EDMs get the balance right.

Accurately Assess Employee Capabilities

If you had packed for a Maui beach vacation and then were given the opportunity to trek the Himalayas, you would obviously need to repack. You'd swap your swimsuit and flip-flops for parkas and hiking boots. But you'd keep your toothbrush and some of your T-shirts in the bag. That decision-making process is similar to what you need to do when sending people on a development journey. Your first task is to help people understand what's in their skill "suitcase" that can be of value in the new role. Then consider what they might unpack and what they may be missing for the next destination. Here's how Jared thought about helping Sheila pack the right stuff for a new development journey:

> Plant manager Jared wanted to move Sheila, the plant controller, one step closer to learning the skills to become a plant manager in the future. His plan? To expand her role to include quality management (QM). This objective worked very well with the QM function's recently adopted approach of empowering front-line supervisors to improve quality. Jared thought about Sheila's biggest strengths: an almost reflexive action to jump in and solve problems independently, and her highly developed skill of digesting and interpreting the numbers. For her new quality management role, Sheila wouldn't need to lean on her number-crunching skills, so that could be left out of her "suitcase." Similarly, she

could unpack her skill of solving problems on her own. Sheila would need to add some new skills to her luggage, including superior questioning and listening skills to find out what supervisors needed to learn about quality, developing rapport to gain credibility, and teaching ability to help others understand how to use QM data.

When you are assessing skills to develop your staff, remember that it really helps to push yourself to be specific. Don't just think "communication skills." Get inside that broad notion and identify the behaviors as you have seen people apply them on the job or how you would like to see them applied in an expanded work setting. For example, a better phrasing than "You have poor communications skills" would be "You are good at listening but too wordy in replying to people. To progress in a broader role, you will need to be able to present ideas in a meeting succinctly, without drawing out your explanations."

Articulate What Is to Be Learned, Not Just What Needs to Get Accomplished

The picture of what people need to learn in a new assignment may be clear in your mind. It's less likely that the picture is as clear in their minds. If the lessons inside the assignments are not crystal clear, you run the risk that people will rely heavily on their familiar skills to get the job done and miss the chance to grow new skills. Consider this story about a manager who at first failed to make development goals clear:

Hector was a division VP of a Fortune 100 company who had been tracking Jim, a bright and likable high flyer in the Finance Department, for ten years. Hector liked what he saw. During many assignments on several division and corporate strategic initiatives, Jim consistently turned out innovative ideas and good plans to implement those ideas. Hector quietly identified Jim as his heir apparent. But Jim needed some rounding out, so Hector sent him off to head up the León, Mexico, operation for a couple of years.

At first, Jim focused on making great improvements in the back office rather than dealing with plant operations. He felt that his cultural and language difference might upset the flow. He essentially relied on his plant staff to keep things humming. The locals loved him, and Jim had a sense of pride for having mastered the role of general manager. But Hector saw that Jim had missed the primary learning goal. With some help from his HR partner, Hector acknowledged his fault of not clarifying the development goal and caught his own misstep just in time. On a visit to León, he sat with Jim and clarified what Jim needed to learn from the assignment in order to develop as a GM: how to create a market-based strategy with his staff and then help them align their goals to that strategy. Jim also needed to learn how to lead cross-culturally.

That conversation made all the difference. The goals were clear and the needs identified. Together, Hector and Jim came up with some specific developmental support options that included setting Jim up with a mentor, a general manager who had successfully implemented strategies in different cultures.

How might you clarify learning goals in your workplace? For example, you might assign an individual contributor the lead role on a project team and tell her you want her to get experience running a team. But don't stop there. "Running a team" is too soft a target. She might interpret that to mean that she should guide others in the use of her well-honed project management skills. You, on the other hand, may want her to gain skill in managing conflict and in group decision making. You don't want her to end up "doing more of the same instead of getting the gain." When you are crystal clear with employees, they have the direction they need to adjust their behaviors. You will end up spending your time on the right conversations. They will be less likely to fall into the same old rut and more likely to accept your feedback as they lean into the discomfort of learning new ways to operate.

Assign Work That Stretches but Does Not Overwhelm

When you stretch a muscle, you're actually creating tiny tears that heal and make the muscle stronger. Stretch it too much, and you rip it, causing pain and perhaps necessitating surgery. Ouch!

Similarly, assigning work that stretches is a balancing act. Not enough stretch, and there's little development. Too big a stretch, and the assignment can backfire, hurting people in the process. EDMs caution that you don't want anyone (or yourself) to have to deal with the blowback that comes from serious performance shortfalls. It will break your heart if a good employee fails publicly, gets taken off an assignment, or receives a lower performance rating. Too much unsupported and unmonitored stretch may break a person's career.

Here is where your careful assessment of capabilities pays off. Consider how one manager thought through the right amount of stretch for an employee:

> Gerald, a program tester in a software company, wanted to be a program manager NOW. Carly, his boss, knew that Gerald had shown some key management qualities, such as being able to orient new testers and be the "go to" person for people who were learning the ropes. But at the same time, she felt it would

be too big a step to move him directly into a management role. Instead, she carved out a new part-time role for him. While he spent 70 percent of his time as a tester, he also had a project to lead. This project assignment (leading a task force to improve the initial training and assimilation of new testers) built on his strengths. It gave Gerald the opportunity to hone his project management skills without the intense pressure of managing a time-sensitive and higher-risk software project.

This vignette is an example of a half-step that stretches the employee without the risks of a full-step job change. Half- or even quarter-steps take many forms. Can you spot opportunities to encourage employees to question the status quo, to give them assignments as members of a task force, or to position them as a mentors to others? How about giving people greater decision-making responsibilities, the challenge of filling in for a supervisor, or the responsibility to handle a high-risk stakeholder interface for a certain period of time?

Although the balance between safety and risk is often hard to judge at the outset, give it your best shot and then stay tuned. We found that even EDMs experience backfires when they neglected to watch employees' stretch assignments closely enough. No matter how much stretch you build in—a little or a lot—monitor and adjust the assignment to keep the development tension just right. Look for early warnings of stretch strain, and be prepared to intervene. Expect to make early adjustments, especially if you have built in a lot of stretch.

3. Seize Developmental Moments

What do you think would happen if we asked a totally stressed-out manager to take an hour out of her busy day to meditate? She just might reach over her desk and throttle us. So instead we suggested that she take two minutes every now and then to stand up and concentrate on breathing in and out. She actually tried it—to great effect. Likewise, EDMs find that there's time for development when they are creative about putting small pieces of development into the crevices of a busy day—their staff's and their own. To EDMs, development just naturally feels like moments in between other stuff. They don't see or experience development as an extra activity requiring meetings, complex forms, or awkward discussions. To them—and maybe to you—these extras feel like distractions from work. Stay out of the trap of distractions by viewing development as moments that occur "inside the job" of getting results. You'll find that development becomes manageable and doable.

Let's look at some ways that EDMs make development moments happen.

Look for Moments to Help Staff Develop a More Strategic View

Because having the big picture in mind helps people work smarter, EDMs find ways to show employees how to climb up to see the higher-level view. One EDM simply took the time to share information about the total business in one-on-one and staff meetings. She described this approach as "getting them attached to the business as well as their jobs." Another had people attend meetings to gain exposure to corporate decisions. He called it "getting out of the cheap seats." How about having people interview the creators and keepers of growth-driving initiatives? Even having people read and discuss the annual report can do wonders for understanding the strategy and financial drivers of the business.

Open Eyes to New Approaches

We find that EDMs like to "get Socratic." This questioning approach works well for people who need to discover new ways to operate, particularly if they are using the wrong ones or are new to the team. Adopt your own version of the Socratic method by asking questions to help employees think and act differently. For example, an EDM we'll call Ken knows that a direct report, Sharon, needs to deal with an irritable stakeholder. Instead of offering advice, a natural tendency, he asks her questions that help her see it from the customer's perspective. With another of Ken's direct reports, Chad who is trying new ways to develop customer relationships with the major decision makers, Ken asks him questions about what worked and why and what didn't and why. Question-driven discussions can be short—even passing encounters in the hallway. EDMs keep their solutions and advice in the background and position them later in the discussion. For example, they lead with questions such as "What resources might be useful to address your current challenge?" and only later suggest something like "I would tend to do this. What do you think?"

Powerful questions, well crafted, lead to even deeper conversation and learning. Questions can uncover assumptions, challenge the status quo, and take your employee into new territory. EDMs have told us that to be most positive and productive, how they ask the question is key. Diana Whitney, a renowned expert on the art of positive questioning that leads to productive results, has written a dozen books on this topic! The three parts to what she calls an "appreciative question" are letting others know the importance of the question or conversation, a rapport-building lead-in that conveys a sincere invitation for the other person's response, and a ready string of probes to uncover their best thinking.[5]

Satisfy Appetites for Lots of Feedback

EDMs know that everyone needs and benefits from instant feedback. Yes, people really do want "the good, the bad, and the ugly" as soon as you see it. There has been much talk about how Gen Xs and Ys want and need your feedback. But it's a universal desire among people of all generations. Regardless of age, all the exceptional developing employees (EDEs) that we talked with put feedback near the top of the list of developmental practices they most value in managers. One said, "I am passionate about my work and want to grow. I've only had one real developmental manager. She took the time to give me feedback—constantly. Both positive and negative. And it made all the difference."

 Tool Kit
The Feedback Formula

- » Give feedback soon: immediacy makes an impression.
- » Focus on behaviors, not personality. That way, it's not too hot to handle.
- » Take advantage of times you can recognize good behavior and performance—this, too, is learning.
- » Don't confuse feedback with "getting something off your chest."
- » Learn to read each individual to know the right amount of feedback to deliver. Avoid giving too much. Some people can take a lot; others need it in bite-size pieces for it to be effective.
- » Stay open to new information. Be loose enough to change your point of view.
- » Always give feedback privately, out of the earshot of others. Otherwise, the discussion will shut down fast.

Merle, an EDM who told us she considers development part of her job, explains her use of feedback as follows: "I approach development as an everyday, 'being there' sort of thing, not a programmatic process. If I see something, I address it; I don't wait for a meeting." She stays conscious not only of task completion but also of the way in which tasks are done. What is important is that the method moves the needle forward for the next time. In many instances, a few minutes is all it takes for Merle to provide feedback. It's just a way of managing for Merle, and it doesn't take lots of extra time. And because the lucky people she manages get smarter and more productive, Merle saves time by not needing to do as much corrective coaching, people shuffling, and other time-wasting tasks.

Turn Mistakes into Instant Learning

EDMs don't mind mistakes if people are open to learning from them. A story about Jack Welch told by Ram Charan provides a memorable example of how to turn a mistake into a development opportunity. Welch was sitting in on a demonstration of e-commerce when the computer equipment failed. The middle-level manager running the show was mortified. What did Welch do? He looked at the group and asked, "If this happened in front of a customer, how would it have felt? What would you have done in that situation?" He knew that the presenter had rehearsed and prepared. Pouncing on him would have been cruel, but ignoring the glitch would have been a wasted opportunity for learning. Welch showed how elegant and easy it was to make it a learning moment.[6]

Keep the Right Distance

Don't think that promoting employee independence means you are missing in action. Quite the contrary. EDMs stay in the picture. They listen to frustrations, ask thought-provoking questions, encourage employees to keep trying, and help identify resources. They try to avoid parachuting in to perform a rescue. But at the same time, they are not bystanders to crash-and-burn situations. An EDE who reports to EDM Lori (the manager mentioned in the beginning of the Introduction), enthusiastically told us, "Lori pushed me out on the ledge. It was scary and exhilarating. But I knew she quietly had my back the whole time."

Sometimes nothing is more motivating for employees than the threat of failure. Often this high-stakes atmosphere leads to great learning and breakthroughs and helps employees build confidence and resilience. The next time they encounter a troubling situation, they will be less likely to back down. Eventually, they will approach obstacles with greater fortitude. But proceed with caution. As with stretch assignments, your distance is a balancing act. If you prefer to get things done right and get them done quickly, this approach to promoting autonomy may be tough for you to take. You might be inclined to get in too close and end up overprotecting people when they could achieve deep development from the threat of potential failure.

4. Leverage Team Learning

You can get development "wholesale," getting more for less. We found that most EDMs excel at adapting the approaches we've outlined for individuals to entire teams of people on a wholesale basis. They didn't sacrifice results. They found a way to get development while getting results and leverage the wholesale benefits of the team structure. The overall outcome: an incredible developmental multiplier.

Want some ideas for how to achieve that multiplier? Think simply of three times three. Three actions you take with your team to do at each of three stages: the beginning, middle, and end. You'll recognize the team-size application of many of the same techniques we have covered in this chapter.

Manage the Beginning, as You Start Working on a New Effort Together

First, Establish a Developmental Culture from the Get-Go

EDMs make it abundantly clear from the very start that they expect both learning and result outcomes. That message sets the right tone for teams. When EDMs constantly ask questions about what people are learning and how that learning can be applied, they reinforce the development culture. And when they publicly commend people for using those lessons, they further establish the development-focused work environment.

Second, Set Out Clear Work Assignments with Room for Learning

Teams learn best when they have an important task that is outside their immediate grasp. That stretch creates both the room and necessity for learning. You want them to struggle a bit but not get lost in the wilderness. Providing the rules of engagement up front really helps them avoid veering off track. Take a page from EDM Frank, who says, "I clearly charter the teams with the business objectives and the mission. I also provide the ground rules, boundaries, and budget." Because Frank provides "guard rails," he can give teams big and slightly terrifying goals and be confident that they will learn their way into meeting these goals.

Third, Staff the Team Developmentally

Think in terms of staffing the team with "shorts" and "longs" of experience. EDMs make sure the team has the sum of smarts it needs while also providing opportunities for those who are there primarily to learn. Here's one variation from Fred, the CEO of a midsize software development firm: "I often use teams developmentally. I mix pros with people who need to learn things in order to contribute to the team's goals. I inform the teams of their core mission, available resources and score card targets. I also let them know their decision-making authority and how I expect them to share information."

Here's another approach from EDM Kay: "I like putting people on cross-functional teams so they can see different styles, approaches, and skills in motion. And I make it clear that this learning is a requirement in addition to results."

Manage the Middle, Once Team Members Are in a Rhythm of Working Together

First, Don't Hover but Be Near

EDMs toe the line between staying out of the way of teams and remaining close enough to respond to calls for help or sense when they should intervene. Here's how Phillip works the balance: "I get out of the way of the teams I have set up, but I create a way for the team to call me in if I'm needed." Betty summarizes her approach this way: "I would give the team stretch goals and encourage team members to lean into the learning. They knew I would not judge them as not measuring up as they struggled to fill gaps in learning. I also watched over my shoulder, but not too closely, to do things like run interference, negotiate for resources, and position them well with senior managers, who were sometimes too nervous about results."

Second, Use Questions to Spur Learning

When EDMs do appear on the team scene, they ask questions instead of giving answers. Brad describes his team visits like this: "I spend most of my time asking questions that clarify thinking, cause the team to consider options, lay out different scenarios, or help people think through reactions of key stakeholders. Often my questions generate additional requirements for information and analysis to get to the bottom of complex issues. And if someone makes a mistake, I use questions to turn it into a learning opportunity."

Third, Add Learning Resources and Subtract Distractions

Sometimes teams need access to information or to people with knowledge and experience. EDMs keep the learning on track by connecting teams with what they need. One manager set up brown bag lunches where experts shared ideas. Another brought in some reports that added new perspective. This technique is a matter of putting the right learning resources in the path of the team at the right time—when team members are stuck or when they need to broaden perspectives.

Learning takes time and energy. EDMs tend to run interference for teams so that the teams don't have to spend time on busywork or dealing with people who waste their time. Of course, there's a balancing act here, too. Be careful not to go too far and insulate teams from people who are difficult but are also key players. Much can be learned by figuring out how to work with challenging experts and stakeholders—as you'll see in Chapter 4.

Manage the End, When Teams Are Winding Down Their Efforts

First, Gather Feedback About the Team

Teamwork, particularly when it's developmentally stretching, is all-consuming. Sometimes there's not a minute to step back and look at how the team is doing. So timely feedback about how the team's actions are perceived by others and how others are being affected by the team's results can be extremely valuable. We've seen teams put together an online survey to collect feedback. Others have pulled together a mini-project for team members to go out and briefly interview others to find out reactions. There are many creative ways to get this additional envelope of information—and it provides a nice chunk of perspective to bring into a project debrief (we'll get to that in a minute).

Second, Insist on Postimplementation Team Learning

In the middle of the team process, the opportunity is to learn in the moment. At the end, after key milestones have been completed, the opportunity is to learn from reflection. Many workers have little patience to reflect on learning once projects are completed. We're all too eager to go to the next challenge. That tendency short-circuits learning and keeps us from reusing it. EDMs follow the example of the CSI TV shows, which always include postmortems in which the characters uncover new layers of learning. One CEO described his process this way: "I insist on postmortems and try to attend as many as I can. We discuss what went wrong and what to learn from it, as well as what went right and how to play that forward."

Third, Institutionalize the Learning

Project debrief meetings signal to teams that you're serious about making talent your business. They're also a sure-fire way to transfer key lessons among the team members. The idea here is to institutionalize the learning. EDM Scott shared this insight: "I always take time to talk about what the team learned. If I don't, the next time I task a team with development and results goals, I will not be taken seriously. Plus, these conversations are fun and inspiring for me."

Consider This
Tips for Leading a Project Debrief

» Communicate the purpose of the debrief: encapsulate learning to apply going forward.

» Ask people to come prepared by bringing their best insights and feedback.

» Bring people together as soon as possible after the end of the project, while memories are fresh.

» Pick an appropriate place, set aside enough time, and set the tone for open and free-ranging discussion with input from all. The debrief meeting isn't the same as a celebration in a bar or on the golf course.

Four Key Questions to Guide the Project Debrief with Team Members

» Did we get the results we planned for? If not, how did our results differ from our expectations?

» What factors and team behaviors had the greatest impact on the results?

» What are the primary lessons learned from this team effort?

» What would we do differently in the future as a result of this effort and project review?

Export Learning

After-action reviews certainly turn up the heat on learning. To make the learning even more valuable, many EDMs require teams to export learning to others outside the team. Often they contribute to that effort by putting team members on a management team agenda or setting up other opportunities for them to share. The very act of sharing hard-won lessons puts a multiplier effect on what was learned: when the learning is passed on to others who would not otherwise have access to this new know-how, more people have benefited than those initially involved.

Be sure to incorporate these developmental practices in your approach to teams. If you do, you will be well on your way to creating what Lynda Gratton calls "hot spots"—teams that are full of energy and innovation because you engage them in complex work that captures their imagination. As she points out, "The latent energy that you and others have is much more likely to be sparked if the task you are engaged in is complex, ambiguous, and difficult."[7]

▶ Case in Point ◀

Bob was an operations executive in a fast-growing company pioneering a new business model in the risk management industry. With no candidates in the local employment marketplace skilled to do new jobs such as counseling consumers when their identity was stolen, he had no choice but to staff his team with bright and hardworking but relatively inexperienced people. His challenge was to get results fast in order to grow the business while also providing lots of development for the newbies on his team.

Enter Maria, a high-potential twenty-something member of Bob's team. With a true gift for customer service, Maria, who started as the first customer care professional, was promoted to be the manager of the small but growing department of consumer counselors. She was a fast learner and a good judge of people. But she was also tough enough to hold people accountable for results and good at coaching new counselors.

Bob knew he had to help Maria do her current job as well as become prepared for the expansion of her team as the numbers of customers grew rapidly. Bob kept in close touch with her as she started managing people. He used his daily encounters with her to help her quickly tackle increasingly complex challenges, such as interfacing with top executives in order to close sales with new customers. Bob says, "I abhor micromanaging. I do my best to make measurable success criteria as clear as possible to staff. I say, 'Here's how I define success. I will not be mad if you use your own judgment or if you do it differently than I would. We'll talk about it.'"

Bob used clearly defined results to anchor Maria's learning. Working on skills to fill the gaps was the development plan. In addition to the issue-driven daily encounters that provided great instant learning opportunities, Bob also set aside time for longer weekly one-on-one meetings.

Even with all this support, Maria "lost it" during one stretch task when the sales vice-president promised a customer something Maria knew couldn't be delivered. She started arguing with the sales VP in front of the customer.

Turning the mistake into a lesson, Bob asked Maria what else she could have done to deal with the situation. This process helped Maria channel her passion for the customer into more politically effective responses.

This example is characteristic of Bob's development style. He says, "It's my job to teach my staff how to maintain a professional demeanor when they get upset. They can blow off steam in my office; then we talk about the appropriate way to react. I give them ideas to practice in order to be more professional young managers." This case demonstrates how Bob "makes every day a development day." He tucks development right into the work, creates the right stretch, supports that stretch, and nudges development along through his regular on-the-spot coaching.

Key Points for Making Every Day a Development Day

▶▶ Tuck development into employees' work. Find creative ways to keep adding stretch to people's work so they develop more *while* getting better results.

▶▶ Design assignments with just the right amount of stretch by starting with an accurate assessment of current capabilities and then communicating clearly what needs to be learned.

▶▶ Find and act on daily opportunities to develop new skills. Keep some distance and encourage independence, yet be close enough to help your employees persist in the face of obstacles.

▶▶ Consider the team a treasure trove of development opportunities. Set team development goals, mix expertise of staff members, and expect and support transfer of learning.

chapter 2 *Tap the Psychological Side of Development*

"WHAT? YOU EXPECT ME TO BE AN AMATEUR PSYCHOLOGIST?" That's what we often hear from anxious clients when we discuss some of the core skills involved in making talent your business. Our answer? "Well, yes. If you want to make a deeper developmental impact with your employees, you can't be just logical. You also need to be psychological." Often managers think that laying out performance directives and instructing team members to "try new approaches" leads directly to achievement of development goals. Guess what? That doesn't work.

Maybe like other managers, you glaze over when someone starts talking about psychological approaches. They are the fuzzy, soft side of doing business, far removed from the comfort zone of hard numbers and measurable customer deliverables. Addressing the "soft stuff" may indeed be the hardest part of your job. Yet exceptional development managers (EDMs) who pay attention to the psychological side of development know that this investment of their insight and energy gives them an essential edge in developing talent. In fact, they would feel totally stymied if directed to develop their staff without addressing their staff's "internal processes" such as motivation and self awareness. By recognizing the importance of these approaches and honing your ability to tap into them, you can leverage the time you spend developing your staff, have more of an impact, and get deeper, more sustainable results than if you remain only in the tactical world. Bringing out your inner psychologist really is a vital part of making talent your business.

One of the biggest "a-ha's" from our research was that both EDMs and exceptional developing employees (EDEs) emphasized the importance of the psychological factor even though we didn't ask about it. This pervasive factor cut across all five practices exceptional managers used for development. It took a variety of forms, many of which you'll recognize as strategies you already use. EDMs expressed it in these ways:

+ "Development: it's all about the relationship you build with staff."

+ "They need a safety net to take those really big steps while testing out new skills."

+ "Pushing them to their limit can be overwhelming, yet doing that produces significant breakthroughs."

+ "When they are particularly frustrated, I buoy them up."

On the other side of the equation, EDEs described what they appreciated in their managers with phrases such as

+ "Building my confidence"

+ "Providing a safe place to discuss issues"

+ "Listening to me when I hit a brick wall"

+ "Exploring what was in me that was holding me back"

How to Tap the Psychological Side of Development

Imagine that you've just spent three months finishing your basement. The moment of truth arrives for you to showcase your work to family and friends, many of whom lent a hand. You lead the crew down the dim stairs, and with excitement and anticipation, you flip the light switch. A sigh of disappointment surrounds you as only half of the lights come on. All that work, but without the essential feature of fully wired lighting, there's no way to see the room's details. Your unveiling lost all of its impact, and you feel demoralized.

Developing members of your team can feel just like that. You sink tons of effort and resources into coaching, online tutorials, and specially designed stretch assignments, and they come across simply as more "to-do's" because the connection hasn't been properly "wired." By tapping into a bit of psychology, EDMs help their employees make the essential connections that lead to growth. They help employees understand the link between their emotions and their behavior, between their inner obstacles and their hesitancy to change, between dips in their performance and uncomfortable situations, just to name a few. Helping employees make these connections "wires" them to extend their true potential in a way that deepens and broadens their capabilities.

As a manager, you too are in the enviable position of helping people make these connections every day. If your employees aren't open or ready to learn something new, your energy is wasted—even if they are the smartest bunch around. Your psychological insights open the door for them to pursue more significant and lasting behavior change and growth. The four main approaches you can use to encourage openness that leads to growth are

1. Start with yourself

2. Cultivate relationships built on trust

3. Help employees "see" themselves during key interactions

4. Connect the dots between emotions and learning

1. Start with Yourself

EDMs we talk to know that the first step in tapping into the psychological side of development is looking in the mirror. Taking a cue from the adage "Master, know thyself," these astute managers (brave enough to look in the mirror without blinking) improve their own self-awareness before asking employees to improve theirs.

We know that increasing your own self-awareness involves some hard work. We assure you, however, that it will deliver huge dividends. The very process of becoming self-aware opens you up to what it takes for others to develop their self-awareness. You'll practice pausing to recognize your emotional state, observing how you behave under stress, identifying how you deal with trade-offs, recognizing your strongly held beliefs that color your decision making, and so forth. When you are courageous enough to look at your own strengths and weaknesses, triumphs and defeats, you'll be in a better place to empathize with your employees. Like Jake in the next story, you can even become a positive role model rather than a distant demanding boss.

At a staff meeting, Jake, a thoughtful systems operations manager, shared the story of how he got a difficult internal client to move ahead with a plan that had been stalled. A few weeks earlier, some of the staff had been at the meeting during which the frustrated internal client had put a major project in jeopardy. Incensed, she threatened to let the VP of finance know how much the lack of progress with the new system was costing the company. In recapping the situation for his staff, Jake explained his initial reaction: "I knew I was ready to jump all over this client. It was her insistence on grandfathering the old system that was causing all our delays and cost overruns. My first instinct was to let her have it. But in a flash of insight, I realized opening my mouth at that point would really set us back. I stopped myself in my tracks and simply told her we wanted to find a win-win. I asked her to meet later in the day to discuss ideas to move forward.

"With my head pounding, I went to think this through with Christy. Many of you know she is a colleague whose opinion I really trust. Christy helped me realize I was creating my own roadblock with our client by not really delving into her true objective for grandfathering. The point was that she didn't want to make her users have to jump through a lot of hoops during the year-end closing. I realized two other things. First, I had been too hell-bent on getting this installation over and done with. I wasn't really being flexible. Second, although this client probably doesn't even know it, she whines a lot. That can really set me off. So I told myself that I would not let the whining get to me. Instead, I wrapped my head around the best way to give her the 'old user-friendliness' she needed to get over the year-end hump. We met at three o'clock and smoothed everything out. She got what she wanted, and so did we. So that's how we got back on track. It was all about me changing my attitude and

*reaction, not about blaming or changing her. In the end, it all
worked out."*

Jake did a stellar job in the self-awareness department. By paying attention to his headache, Jake realized he would not be operating at his best to handle a sensitive client situation. In reaching
out to talk with a trusted colleague, he gained perspective on his
own somewhat dysfunctional behavior. He developed insight into
how the client triggered some negative reactions in him. And by
sharing his story with his team, he became a role model in using
self-awareness to turn a situation around. Way to go, Jake.

Success stories like this reflect research that shows that self-
awareness correlates even more strongly with leadership success
than IQ and technical skills, which are often thought of as more
important. This big idea may remind you of Daniel Goleman's
groundbreaking work on emotional intelligence that made such
a stir in the business world of the mid-1990s.[1] Your success as
a leader and your power to develop both revolve around your
understanding of the impact of your emotions on performance
and relationships. When you demonstrate self-awareness, you
can operate more transparently and share your thoughts more
freely; in so doing, you implicitly invite others to similarly reveal
their "true selves." The more you are able to tune into your own
motives and emotions, the more you can help employees understand and explore their own.

 ## Consider This
Background on Emotional Intelligence

Think of your emotional intelligence (EI) quotient as
having these four components: self-awareness, self-
management, social awareness, and relationship manage-

ment. The first component lays the foundation for the rest. Here are signs that you are well on your way to mastering self-awareness and self-management.

Capability for self-awareness shows up this way:

» You can recognize your feelings (such as anger or embarrassment) as they happen. This is not always so easy to do because you are likely in a "thinking" mode. When you recognize the feeling, you are no longer at its mercy. For example, a self-aware person would be able to say, "This conversation is not going well. I'm feeling frustrated. I can now see that this happens every time this client suggests we bring in additional team members to help us out, simply because we hit a temporary obstacle. I find that a bit insulting."

» You use certainty about your feelings to make better decisions about next steps. For example, "Every time I feel backed into a corner, I realize I am upset about not having my point of view heard. I'd better find a reasonable way to get my ideas into the conversation."

Capability for self-management shows up this way:

» You have emotional self-control and can delay gratification. For example, a self-managing person would say, "I am super-eager to move ahead on my plan, but I see folks have too many questions that need attention first."

» You demonstrate transparency and adaptability. For example, "I will let my team know how the new direction from management caused my favorite project to get derailed. And even though that hurts, I can move forward with management's plan because I see such promise in it."

» You are able to shake off emotions of anxiety or gloom rather than wallow in them. For example, shaking off emotions might sound like this, "Oh, no, they are asking us to adapt a new platform right in the middle of our implementation with this client! OK, we will find a way to keep the implementation going while we respond to the new platform, even if I need to bring in a few extra hands this month."

2. Cultivate Relationships Built on Trust

Many managers believe their employees trust them. But our research showed that while most managers think they are doing OK in the trust department, EDEs would like their managers to be better at building trust. This dichotomy is crucial because trust is an essential ingredient for making talent your business. Over the past few decades, we've become more aware of the fall-out from trust gaps in organizations.

In workplaces in which employees don't trust management, cooperation suffers and adaptability in the face of marketplace changes screeches to a halt. Posturing prevails, rumors run rampant, and what people really think goes underground. Faced with a forest of hidden agendas and people playing it safe to get by, managers end up being consumed by resolving misunderstandings and tensions between people, rather than making real progress toward goals. Sound familiar? If so, you know that it's simply exhausting to work in a low-trust environment. As Dennis and Michelle Reina describe in their book *Rebuilding Trust in the Workplace*, low trust saps not only energy but also confidence and commitment.[2] And you need all three in large quantities to develop talent and generate high performance.

But when employees trust you, your ability to help successfully expand their skills increases immeasurably. According to the Reinas' research, trust gives people the confidence to take risks and change their behavior[3]—both prerequisites for learning and development. Think of trust as a condition for creating collaborative capital that enhances both relationships and results. For example, your staff member may not be willing to try a new business tool because a sales rep sings its praises, but if a trusted colleague says it would add tremendous value for the work he's doing, your staff member is likely to get right on board.

Trust is also a prerequisite for effective feedback, the "breakfast of champions" for fueling new development. Why would your staff take feedback from someone whose motives they don't trust? When trust is present in your relationship, your employees will be willing to listen to and learn from your feedback, whether it stings or it sings. Their trust in you provides a safety net for the vulnerability that comes with new self-awareness. With their trust, you can expect more loyalty, commitment, and growth.

Even though it is an essential skill, building trust with employees isn't in your job description and probably wasn't covered in any management course you've taken. How, then, do you find the time and path to reinforce or repair trust? Through paying attention to your own behavior every day, so that over time you build the three types of trust outlined by the Reinas.

The first is contractual trust: fulfill obligations and commitments without exceptions. If you make an offer to a staff member, you need to follow through—no empty promises. Be consistent, delegate appropriately, and encourage mutually serving intentions.[4]

Second, build communication trust by being honest, sharing information, and maintaining confidentiality.[5] Telling a staff member half-truths about the virtues of a project assignment or withholding important details jeopardizes not only the development opportunity but also your relationship.

Third, practice competence trust. Acknowledge people's needs, skills, and abilities, and support them in making their own decisions.[6] For example, if a big new assignment makes it difficult for your employee to respond to family obligations, acknowledge this tension and support the person in finding effective remedies.

Your people will notice what you do to build trust. An EDE we'll call Elaine shared this story with us:

> Elaine was thrilled to have a new development opportunity in the form of playing junior partner to a more seasoned financial professional. But not everyone was happy about this arrangement. At a management meeting, two other managers ranted publicly about the potential risk factors. Rather than back down to pressure, her trust-building manager, Henry, took on the concerns one by one and made sure the potential exposures were addressed. Although the assignment was delayed while Henry put all the pieces into place, in the end, Elaine's relationship with Henry was transformed by the experience. Having witnessed Henry going to bat for her, she knew she could truly trust Henry as her manager and as a person. As a result, Elaine's tenacity to work through roadblocks increased, as did her willingness to go the extra mile in producing great results while learning new skills.

The benefits of building trust are not confined to the lines linking you and your staff members. By experiencing a trusting relationship with you, your employees learn about the power of trust in their other relationships. Their payback for doing this will be huge. Each trusting relationship they build multiplies the number of their relationships that can be developmental for them. Sometimes there is nothing more powerful and helpful than having your staff member hear feedback (solicited or unsolicited) from a trusted colleague. In fact, impressive EDEs have articulated the power this way: the more trusting the relationship, the more important that relationship becomes in building confidence and encouraging them to take on calculated risks. One professional told us, "Closeness really matters. When there is less of it, there is less learning because the trust is not there." Likewise, EDMs value how others can provide emotional support to their employees, sometimes in ways they cannot. They therefore encourage their people to build a network of strong relationships that foster growth.

3. Help Employees "See" Themselves During Key Interactions

"The unexamined life is not worth living." This powerful observation, stated centuries ago by Socrates, has been expanded upon by Warren Bennis, who has invested over five decades to promoting sage leadership practices: "The unexamined life is impossible to live successfully. Like oarsmen, we generally move forward while looking backward, but not until we truly see the past—truly understand it—can we truly move forward and upward."[7] By being the agent who helps people see their behavior and link it to their future actions, you inspire the personal growth that underpins successful professional development.

Encouraging self-reflection is not intended to be a therapy session. Instead, it's about guiding your employee to explore what is "inside" (behind his or her behavior) and what is "outside" (how his or her behaviors truly affects others). "Doing what comes naturally" without examining what's beneath the surface and ignoring how others experience the interaction can be risky. Operating in panic mode, bullying others who are not keeping pace, and flirting to get a work favor are employee actions that backfire. Your staff members, often caught up in the pressure to achieve results, can fall into such behaviors and be completely unaware of their impact. They are doing what they have been conditioned to do, what they watched their families of origin do, or what they ingeniously developed as a survival habit.

Most managers are certainly not equipped to try to uncover the complexities of each person's psychological drivers, and there's no need to. Instead, EDMs simply hold up a mirror for their employee in a way that provides perspective—both about the assumptions that are driving that behavior and the downsides of acting in that way.

 Good Ideas . . .
For Holding Up a Mirror

Holding up a mirror so that an employee can see his behavior and its impact doesn't take an advanced degree in psychology. It can be as simple as asking the right questions *after* an event. Try these:

» How did you feel as you were approaching that situation?

» What assumptions were behind the choices you made in that discussion?

» What approaches did you use to manage or modify the situation?

» What impact did your actions have on others?

When you ask such questions with care and often enough, you will help increase his reflective skills and also encourage him to seek your feedback after events so that he will learn more about himself more quickly.

Once he has a read on his current behaviors, use these questions *before* an upcoming event to help him to plan his approach:

» Where are you feeling least confident in your approach to these interactions?

» At the upcoming client meeting, how will you make the client feel truly heard?

» Where do you think it is most likely you'll make a mistake? How can you avoid that?

» What approaches can you use to help you gain client buy-in?

Pose these questions with sincere curiosity, and you will avoid a leading tone that implies you have the "right" answer. These ongoing and insightful questions can help put your employees' self-awareness into high gear.

Keep your eyes open to patterns of ineffective responses to challenging situations. These challenging situations leave your employees feeling vulnerable because they do not have a handy way to respond. If you can engage employees during these tense, difficult moments that cry out for new self-awareness, you can encourage their self-reflection. That will go a long way toward helping them get out of the ditch and onto the higher path of valuable learning. Think about the advantages for yourself and your team. Employees who have taken that higher path are more able to minimize painful situations, push through challenges to achieve better results, and leave you with a lot less cleanup to do.

Four important patterns to watch for every day are emotional outbursts, being stalled by surprises and setbacks, negative reactions to unsolicited feedback, and lack of resilience in the face of obstacles.

Emotional Outbursts

It's human nature to get defensive and justify acting out. But bad things can happen when your employees allow emotions to hijack their conversations and interactions. An occasional outburst under pressure may be forgiven. A recurring pattern, on the other hand, is cause for alarm and a call for you to intervene.

Sometimes you'll meet a wall of defensiveness when you step in. Past experience with this seemingly immovable wall is the reason some managers don't even try to intervene. The wall resonates with excuses like "I was stressed," "He just wouldn't listen," and "She was a jerk." EDMs overcome this obstacle by turning the conversation away from such evasive comments. They help employees see how their emotional and sometimes instinctive, automatic behavior has undermined their effectiveness. In so doing, they help them break a negative cycle.

Can you turn someone around in a single conversation? Unlikely. Instead, plan for a series of conversations with your employee to help her see the pattern over time. Little by little, she will develop a more accurate picture of herself and will seek out a better way. Alternatively, if her defenses are simply too high, have her dissect the behavior of a positive role model—someone who handles situations well. That arm's-length exercise reduces the chance that she will feel judged and opens her mind to consider how she also could make those kinds of behavioral choices.

Being Stalled by Surprises and Setbacks

We all have moments of disappointment or surprise when we find out things aren't going as well as we thought. Most employees can easily navigate the small bumps, but big bumps can stop them in their tracks. They may have missed a cue or two along the way or simply were heads down, getting the work done, and did not notice that they were about to collide with a big problem. EDMs are on the lookout for stalled employees, and when they see one, they step in with a one-on-one chat to soften the blow, lead to a quicker recovery, and create lasting insight. Your work here is to help employees in these situations adjust their attitude after being caught off-guard and help them bounce back from embarrassment or frustration. The work is to examine what happened and move on. The sooner the situation is addressed, the sooner the employees will be back to full steam ahead.

Tool Kit
Reengaging an Employee Stalled by a Setback

A one-on-one conversation to help someone overcome a setback can be as simple as 1-2-3.

1. **Normalize his reasons for frustration or embarrassment**. One manager tells her employees, "Life happens. Despite our best efforts, things go off track" and "Look, you tried something new; that's terrific. You can't get perfection right out of the gate."

2. **Find out what happened**. Do some detective work. If he was expecting one outcome while other team members were expecting something else, where did his

disconnect come from? Were there some missing communications or interactions?

3. **Help him think through the "do-over."** "How can
   you handle it differently the next time?" is a classic
   question that will never go out of style. Of course,
   the setback may have occurred even though he did
   everything right. What then were factors outside of his
   control? Move to the step of helping him gain perspective on the "uncontrollables" and the ways to manage
   himself when these inevitably occur.

Follow this three-part conversation, and you will
encourage your employees to take better steps next time,
rather than acting on their natural desire to avoid such
situations in the future.

Negative Reactions to Unsolicited Feedback

We humans are geared to avoid pain. So isn't it only natural
for employees to avoid unsolicited feedback? When challenged,
it's natural to switch into fight-or-flight mode. What do you
do when one of your employees snaps back or retreats in fear
from the discomfort of feedback? We hope you are not like
Kim, who tells her staff to "just suck it up and get on with your
assignment."

However, a softer version of Kim's approach probably hits
the mark. EDMs help their staff members see their initial reaction, take charge of their emotions, and then get into a place of
actually taking in and using the feedback. A quick conversation
could go something like this: "Yeah, Tom, it stinks when you
get an earful of bad news you didn't ask for from a client. You
just want to walk away. Suppose instead you take a deep breath

and then listen for what might be helpful. Nine times out of ten, the client actually has some helpful nuggets in there."

What Tom may not get is that he risks diminishing his valuable relationship with clients if he gives a negative response to their feedback. They could very well choose in the future to go around him. Tom's continued growth counts on receiving such "gifts" from clients. His ever-improving finesse with clients will necessitate his putting his emotions in check as he listens without judgment and even invites more input and examples.

Lack of Resilience in the Face of Obstacles

When was the last time you got through the month without having to work through a big challenge (looming like a detour sign indicating that the roadway ahead is blocked)? These types of organizational obstacles (such as cutbacks in staff or budget or delays in getting approvals) truly are par for the course and require some specific tactics to address them and "get back en route." When trying new stretch skills or taking on new roles with a project team, your employees will invariably run into obstacles time and time again. This recurring pattern can make your employees, like Juan in the story below, feel particularly vulnerable.

> *Three weeks after Juan assumed his new role as project lead on a matrixed team, he was handed a 30 percent budget and people cut—with no change in the project delivery date. Oww! After going through the stage of disbelief and begging the director for an extension to no avail, he dived into work feverishly, cracking the whip on the project team. Team members witnessed his frustration and disgust on a daily basis. Though the project was finished on time, everyone felt depleted and filled*

with resentment. Juan's workdays had been stretched, but his capabilities were not.

If you had been Juan's manager, what could you have done in this situation?

- Commiserate with Juan. Let him know that you understand how challenging this is and that he's not alone in facing these constraints.

- Help him see the bright spots and understand the implications of his reaction. Remind him of what he has going for himself (self-image) and that others are watching how he, as the project leader, responds to obstacles. Help him see that the leadership quality of resilience is going to be a key to his future success.

- Work with him on identifying some paths out. Ask which tactics would be most effective to address the cutbacks with the same delivery date (for example, negotiating loaned help from another department with the promise to help on that department's work at a later time or rallying the team to "project-plan" this efficiently based on their skill sets).

- Next, turn to his impact on the team. Help him switch gears and transmit a "can do" spirit to the team members. Brainstorm some ways he might lighten the mood through food or fun and ways he could reduce his own stress.

- Be there: let him know your willingness to be on call as his thinking partner. Consider setting up regular meetings just to chat as well as having a truly open door to talk when he needs to.

Your efforts at enhancing self-determination have a substantial psychological impact on how employees approach their work. Studies support this assertion. Dan Pink cites scientific research that being self directed is one the three factors that account for motivation (the other two being mastery and purpose).[8] Employees rise to the occasion and gain a real sense of being capable of getting the job done. As James Kouzes and Barry Posner, authors of the big-selling business book *The Leadership Challenge*, tell us, employees with self-determination will move forward even on difficult tasks because of their deep sense of being in control.[9] Without that feeling of control, these employees show far less commitment to excel. Your coaching can make all the difference in helping them develop resilience.

4. Connect the Dots Between Emotions and Learning

Brandi thought she was going to "lose it." Sometimes she liked the excitement of not knowing what to expect in her new role. Other times she felt terrified. Her brain was on overload. How could she possibly remember one more detail? Every day, there were new people to meet, new ideas to incorporate, and new experiences to absorb. She found that even her yoga class, which usually calmed her down, wasn't enough to soothe her anxiety. By the end of the first week, she felt distraught and almost desperate. But Brandi stuck it out and made it through her initiation into her new assignment.

Within a month, Brandi talked glowingly of this intense period of learning. She described in detail the immense challenge she was feeling to get the assignment done right. "I felt enormous pressure. I did not want to fail at this. But I really lacked much of the right experience for the assignment." In the end, she was able to pull it all together to achieve great results.

The pride on her face was unmistakable as she talked about her first month in her new role.

If you had been Brandi's manager, would you have shielded her from all that stress? Would you have changed your mind and pulled her from the assignment? She might have been more comfortable, but then she wouldn't have come out the other end of this intense experience feeling so positive about herself and her growth.

Stress, emotion, and intensity aren't always bad. They can actually engage us with work and help us learn. Let's take a Discovery Channel approach to tease this one out. Silently, our limbic system processes the incessant input we draw in from external sources and determines which emotional responses will be stored as long-term memory. A song you heard in your teens when your adolescent self was often eagerly happy or dismally sad, in love or in pain, was stored in several places in your brain. That's why your recall of it is so good after all these years: it comes on the radio, and you know every word (much to your children's chagrin!). On the other hand, sensory input with no emotional content is less likely to be passed to long-term memory. So learning that includes an emotional experience (such as fear of failure, the joy of a solution breakthrough, or the hurt of an insult) leads to better memory and, in turn, better development. Dry reading and lecture don't stand a chance compared to emotional experiences.[10]

Think back to a significant learning experience you had at work in the past few years. If you were to recount that learning to a friend, would it include words like scary, disappointing, challenging, or thrilling? Your learning stands out precisely because it has those memorable emotional components. This kind of brain connection underpins the power of stories as a teaching device. People relate to the emotions inherent in a good story, and the information provided becomes much more memorable than simple dry facts.

Whether or not they know this science, EDMs tend to take employees out of their comfort zone to engage them in more complex forms of learning that often require persistence in the face of uncertainty. Letting people try new things on their own, without a step-by-step guide book, ups the risk and therefore the emotional quotient. EDMs do this while accepting some failures as part of the process. And anticipating that their employees will be stressed at times, they plan safe ways or places for them to let the emotions out.

In the end, achievements gained and lessons learned in these circumstances will be the ones that stick and form the backbone of truly deep and broad development—an accumulation of "deep smarts" (described in Chapter 3). While repetitive comfort zone activities require only a limited effort on your part and theirs and produce some results, they do not lead to more enduring development. Remember, however, that it is best if you have a trusting relationship firmly in place before you ask someone to take the plunge into an emotionally charged assignment. One employee we spoke with told us about a "terrifying" assignment in which he thought he would lose his job if he failed. He was overwhelmed and edgy. Yet with his trusted manager just an arm's reach away, he summoned the stamina and resources to achieve a successful outcome. He indicated that it was by far the best development experience he had ever had.

▶ Case in Point ◀

Aaron, an eager investment analyst seeking new opportunities, volunteered spontaneously to step in when a client project was headed for disaster. Then he stepped back and wondered how on earth he would do what his colleague had not been able to do. He anxiously reached out for his manager's help; they already enjoyed a strong and trusting relationship. Aaron's manager, Andy, cautioned him that it would be a big stretch, and the client (the benefits director in an institution investing tens of millions for its retirees) was very demanding and was threatening to take its business elsewhere. Bolstered by his manager's confidence and a relationship built on trust, Aaron entered into these uncharted waters.

The client knew Aaron, but not as the investment team lead. The client needed to be convinced both of his investment savvy and of his ability to be responsive to customers. Wanting to win favor with the client right off the bat, Aaron's interactions with this benefits director were initially overly solicitous. Andy held up a mirror to help Aaron see his behavior and its impact on the client relationship. Aaron took a deep breath and realized that he had to override his strong need to please if he was going to come off as confident. And so it went. Almost every step of the way, the client had some major or minor complaint. Often Andy provided a safety zone from the battlefield. Aaron used this space for thinking through great solutions, identifying other resources, using the client's unsolicited feedback to spur new approaches, and preparing for responding with confidence to the client. At other points, Andy purposely, or out of necessity, let Aaron go it alone.

This assignment was scary. Aaron felt that his career was on the line, and he had many sleepless nights, not just worrying about client demands but also working through the tough and often introspective questions from his boss.

Afterward, Aaron reported, "I learned so much. I hardly had time to process one challenge before another one popped up. This assignment forced me to find my approach and style." He told us how much the experience increased his understanding of his strengths and weaknesses. In the end, the client was satisfied and Aaron's insights were enormous. His reflections regarding what went wrong, what skills needed to be deployed, and how he would handle such a challenge the next time have stayed with him. He often thinks about the way Andy worked with him, causing him to reflect deeply on what was behind his behavior and the effect it had on the client. He values how Andy achieved a balance between pushing him to try new things and being there to talk things through and shore up his confidence. Aaron knows that the way Andy worked with him during those tense months made a major difference in his skills and his career.

Key Points for Tapping into the Psychological Side of Development

▸▸ Become more aware of your own emotional triggers and biases. Significant development starts with self-awareness, and the best way to help others learn self-awareness is to master it yourself.

▸▸ Build trust with your employees. High-trust relationships open the door for the necessarily candid discussions about performance and development, receptiveness to your counsel, and willingness to take risks inherent in learning and behavior change. With trust intact, you give employees a safety net that encourages them to take the leap.

▸▸ Look out for patterns of employee behavior that reveal their emotional blind spots and vulnerabilities. You can use charged events and even mistakes as valuable opportunities for increased self-awareness and a catalyst for trying new behaviors.

▶▶ Act on brain science discoveries about learning. Intentionally provide learning that includes an emotional experience (such as the anxiety of tackling great challenge, the fear of failure, or the joy of a solution breakthrough) so that lessons are more effectively committed to memory and lead to more significant development.

chapter 3 *Connect People with Development Partners*

Our friend Karen participated in her first triathlon this past summer. Early on, her coach, Marty, encouraged her to tap several other colleagues and advisers, but she didn't feel the need to do that. She felt comfortable with all three sports: biking, running, and particularly swimming, which she'd enjoyed over the years. Things went along "swimmingly" until she faced the open bay water for her trial session. Although she was an accomplished pool swimmer, she couldn't get her breathing right in the bay. The experience left her feeling panicky. When Karen shared her discomfort with Marty at her next training session, he reminded her about Chandra, the open-water swimmer he'd recommended she contact months earlier. This time, a highly motivated Karen got together with Chandra. Chandra told Karen, "Bay water currents are tricky. You can't simply turn your head to the side like you do in a smooth pool. Instead, you have to lift your head all the way out of the water as you look forward. That way, you get air and spot your direction. It's a shift that takes a different rhythm and style of breathing." For Karen, this insight made all the difference in the world—so much so that she decided to contact the biking master her coach had recommended. With just three weeks to go before the race, Marty helped her meld the advice of both these lateral coaches into her routines. The result: Karen handled her first triathlon with confidence and placed well, much to her delight.

Exceptional development managers see their role as similar to Karen's triathlon coach. They provide some direct coaching but at the same time bring the right mix of development partners (peers, managers higher in the organization, acknowledged experts) into the picture and then help pull all the learning together so that their employees are prepared to take on challenges with confidence and distinction.

How to Connect People with Development Partners

When it comes to developing staff, have you ever felt overwhelmed by the sheer demand it makes on your time and energy? Relax, help is on the way. Partnering is a practice that lightens your development load and is in fact often the best way to go. Why? When you think of it, much of what we need to learn is already known by others—and those others possibly know more about a specific subject than you. Take the case of a brand-new supervisor who needs to work through the confusion and pain of shifting from being an individual contributor to being a manager who must rely on others. Who might do a better job helping the new supervisor deal with her identity change? Her manager, who went through the transition twenty years ago, or a peer who handled the change effectively within the last two years?

In our study, although exceptional development managers (EDMs) and exceptional developing employees (EDEs) both gave high ratings to the importance of learning from partners as a development strategy that works, EDEs rated it more highly. Research by the Corporate Executive Board reinforces this enthusiastic view. It revealed that learning from others is one of the two top drivers of potential, second only to learning from experience.[1] The following four approaches will help you master the use of development partners and fulfill your employees' desire for this efficient and effective learning tool:

1. Green-light and motivate people to partner up for development

2. Give people an accurate compass to find the right development partners

3. Teach people how to get the most learning from development partners

4. Invest in a network of development partners for the future

1. Green-Light and Motivate People to Partner Up for Development

Jan needed a push to use partners to develop the skills for her new job. She was a talented midcareer professional who moved from a professor role to recruiting new professors for the dynamic university where she had worked for many years. She needed to learn to work with department heads to clarify job descriptions, post jobs on the Internet, qualify candidates, and to make hiring decisions. Jing, the university's vice-president of HR and administration, told Jan, "I'm not the guy to help you learn your new job. The knowledge you need is in our great

*staff. I'll be behind you all the way, and my door is always
open if you want to come in. But here's what I want you to
do. Sit with Jamie. Watch how he plans his day to allocate his
time among tasks such as clarifying specifications, screening
applicants, conducting phone interviews, and doing background
checks. Then sit in on interviews with Lynne. See how she qual-
ifies candidates on the phone. It will give you a great model."*

*Jan listened but was still hesitant. Jing asked, "You aren't
buying this, are you? What's in your way?" Jan replied, "It
feels like I am going around you. You won't be upset, will you?
And the staff are so busy. Won't I be getting in their way?"
Jing laughed. "Jan, I may not know the sophisticated aspects
of recruiting, but I do know two things. Observing, interacting
with, and questioning colleagues, with a good checklist of what
you want to learn in hand, is a great way to learn. I have used
it often in my career. I also know how to create a culture in my
department, where helping new folks learn the ropes is valued
and expected. Jamie and Lynne are on board with the idea of
helping colleagues. Try out my suggestions. You'll see how well
they work."*

Let's face it, many people like Jan think only of you, the
manager, and perhaps their friends, as sources of knowledge and
support. Jan's hesitation reflects what we've often heard: employees think they would be going against protocol or their manager's
wishes if they reach out to other managers or people beyond their
circle of colleagues. EDMs we've seen in action set their employees' minds straight by telling them that it is not just OK but
expected that they reach out to others for development. EDMs
understand that people need permission and motivation to look
in the right places to find the right development partners.

They suggest that the best way to make the permission and expectation concrete for employees is by telling stories showing how powerful learning from development partners can be. This chapter has some stories you can use, but we know you also have great stories in your own experience about times you have learned from others outside your direct reporting relationships. You can make your stories really sing if you remember to include what you learned, who you learned it from, how you learned it, and the impact that partnering with others had on your growth. Nothing sells like success, and personalizing it makes a deep impression.

Adjust your pitch to the learning style of people you're talking with. For example, sell Ted and Barbara, who are more reserved and task-oriented, on how efficient this approach will be for them. If you tell them that setting up their network of development partners the right way will allow them to get *exactly* the learning they need, they will be impressed. Contrast this approach with the one to take with Chip, an energizer bunny who is aggressive and likes to move fast. If you emphasize with him how much faster he'll learn if he's not waiting for you to teach him, he's likely to relate to the value of the approach. For all your staff, you can sell the benefit of the richness of development partners. Having access to a number of people to learn the right things at the right time is simply a more effective way to learn.

2. Give People an Accurate Compass to Find the Right Development Partners

Development partners are potentially everywhere, but how do you help your employees find the right ones? Before you send them off on their search for the right development partners, give them a compass that will point them in the right direction. In this case, the compass is made up of two coordinates, the key questions What? and Who? For best results, you and your employee will need to give careful thought to answering these questions in the right order. Start with the What? coordinate first before lining up the Who?

Start with the *What?*

To get an accurate reading for this coordinate, define the learning goal very clearly and specifically. For example, you might describe the need as

+ Knowledge—such as technical, functional, or customer information
+ Business skills—such as planning and problem solving
+ Interpersonal skills—such as listening, approachability, and making person-to-person connections
+ Leadership skills—such as delegation, giving feedback, and motivating team members
+ Organization savvy skills—such as how to read the political landscape and influence others (see also Chapter 4)

Of course, you will want to be very specific about each learning need. Go beyond the labels, which are really buzzwords, such as "communication," to describe the full thought in whole sentences specific to the person and the situation. In this way, you will make the description very meaningful and link learning to the tasks at hand, which by the way answers another key question, "*Why* learn this?" For example, if you are working on improving the delegating skills of a construction project manager, you might frame it up this way: "Learn how to delegate work scheduling tasks to your construction supervisor so he is more capable and you free up more time to hold meetings with customers." When you help people get crystal-clear about what to learn, you will avoid the common problem of people wandering aimlessly about, unable to figure out whom they need to approach.

If you've done a good job of intentionally planning developmental assignments (as discussed in Chapter 1), you'll have a very good idea of what people need to learn. If you don't have the learning need clearly defined, all is not lost. Check out the simplified conversation in the "Consider This" feature below for a line of questioning you can use to help target the need.

Consider This
A Useful Example for Defining the *What?* Coordinate

Observe how Todd and his manager, Madge, continue a probing discussion until they clearly answer the question "*What* needs to be learned?"

TODD: I want to learn planning skills.

MADGE: Can you *tell me why* you want to learn them?

TODD: I want to be better at planning with my clients.

MADGE: *What are you working on* that has led you to wanting to be better at that skill?

TODD: My project of updating the database for customer care reps is stuck, and I think it is because I don't really understand what they want.

MADGE: It sounds like *the specific planning skill* you are missing is interviewing your clients to determine what they require. Does that sound right?

TODD: Sort of. I do know the questions to ask, but I don't seem to be getting at what they really want. I hear through the grapevine that they think I don't listen and understand their world.

MADGE: Then *one key skill you most likely need* to work on is active listening—probing and testing for understanding of your clients' needs as they see them. Does that sound right?

TODD: Yep, I think that's it.

Now Todd and Madge have the first coordinate of the compass set.

Then Define the *Who?*

Once you and your employee come to agreement on what he really needs to learn, you can start looking together for the Who?—the best person to help him learn it. Generally, employees really need direction from someone who does the What? well, day in and day out, and of course is willing and able to transfer the learning to others. In the Todd and Madge example above, Todd would end up looking for a project manager or a peer who has a knack for using active listening skills with clients.

Finding the person may not be as hard as you think. Keep in mind Aleksandr Solzhenitsyn's observation that "talent is always conscious of its own abundance, and does not object to sharing."[2] Most accomplished people will be very glad to teach or mentor another person, if time and circumstances allow— and if they have some talent in teaching others what they know. If neither you nor your employee has the perfect person in mind, do what the best recruiters do: lay out the "specs" of the person needed to fill the job. With a clear-cut and specific development need defined by the What? both you and your employee can shop for the right person using many avenues both inside and outside the organization. (See an example of how this is done in the "Good Ideas" feature below.)

One thing to keep in mind is the special value of learning from peers. They are not only a source of support, cheerleaders, and a uniquely empathic shoulder, but they also often have golden insights and expertise to share. (The EDEs we talked to were very enthusiastic about learning from peers.) Here are some of their comments on the subject:

- "I tap my peers for learning. Especially when the trust is high, we get beyond layers of protectedness and can share ideas openly."

- "I highly recommend developing personal relationships with colleagues you can learn from. They give you all the juice you need in the world."

- "I get a leg up by learning from my peers. They share what they have learned, and I reciprocate. It's a great way to accelerate our learning."

Good Ideas . . .
For Finding the Right *Who?*

Use online social networking or old-fashioned people-to-people networking to discover willing and capable development partners. Look in the following categories of people to find the right Who?

» **Colleagues** who excel at important skills. For example, peers who have managed a project team or recently moved into supervisory roles can share lessons on how to hold people accountable as well as relay the frustration and challenges of making the switch from an individual contributor to a management role.

» **Managers** or other individuals higher in the organization who have long or broad experience to share, as in how to manage creative people who want freedom to do their own thing so that their output aligns with company goals.

» **Technical people** who understand arcane aspects of the system or product and can explain details the employee doesn't yet understand. For example, they can give tutorials about the engineering concepts underpinning a new product. In so doing, they are likely to educate your employee about the science that lies behind the features.

» **Outsiders** who may not know about your organization but do know a lot about the skill defined in the What? stage. Think broadly. For example, someone struggling with listening may find that a son's guidance counselor has extraordinary skills in developing an easy rapport and using questions to determine students' learning needs.

3. Teach People How to Get the Most Learning from Development Partners

Give permission? Check. Define skills needing development? Check. Development partner defined and recruited? Check. Your job done? Not so fast. Great learning doesn't flow automatically even from the best development partners. There's lots you can teach people in order to turn on that faucet.

Plan for the Complexity of the Learning

EDMs know that different kinds of learning take different kinds of plans. The more complex the "smarts" people need to learn, the more complex the plan, as Georgina found out:

> Georgina landed a new job in the sales support function of a fast growing e-learning business. She had two very different development goals. First, she needed to gain a full understanding of the features of a complicated new product combining content and multiple delivery options. Second, she needed to learn how to share information about the new product with potential early-adopter customers. Carl, her boss, defined these as two learning goals, asking her to craft different approaches for working with the two development partners they chose to help her.
>
> For the product knowledge goal, they determined that a simple sharing of knowledge would do—a bit of technical background to understand how the product works and how to talk about the benefits. Carl suggested, "Georgina, you can probably do this in one or two sessions with Michelle. Just be clear on what you want to know. Read everything you can first about the product, and have a short list of good questions to guide the discussion."
>
> For the second, more complex goal, Carl advised Georgina, "When you meet with Jack, who is a real pro at working with customers, you'll need to structure a longer working relationship to absorb what you need. You'll need to figure out when and how to observe what he does and find some time to talk with him about it. Ideally, it would be great if you could get him to agree to observe you in action, too.
>
> "Of course," he continued, "I'll meet with you to talk about what you are learning and how you can apply it. Sound good?"

Notice how Carl helped Georgina adjust her development partner lesson plans based on the just how complex or how "deep the smarts" were that need to be learned. "Deep smarts" is a concept coined by Dorothy Leonard and Walter Swap to describe more complex, more implicit, hard-to-learn skills. The "Consider This" feature below covers this intriguing concept in more detail and gives tips on how to integrate deep smarts into development plans. The product information Georgina needed to learn was an example of a shallow, simpler learning transfer; the smarts weren't very deep. In contrast, her second development goal, involving approaching early adopters, was deeper learning. It was "softer," more behavioral, and more complicated.

 Consider This
Background on Deep Smarts

In an article in the *Harvard Business Review*, learning researchers Dorothy Leonard and Walter Swap give a theoretical explanation for why learning from development partners is such a high-impact practice.[3] It has to do with what they call "deep smarts," capabilities most desired by people and most valued by organizations. Deep smarts are capabilities such as those that enable people to make intuitive decisions fast, spot problems others miss, and learn how to navigate situations that require a gut sense for interpersonal relationships. These skills are softer, more complex, more implicit and much harder to learn and take a very long time to master.

This theory holds that all but the most technical learning is a result not *just* of training but also of learning on the job and working alongside partners (whom Leonard and Swap call "knowledge coaches"). These are master-apprenticeship relationships. According to Leonard and Swap's research, the deeper the smarts, the more dependent the learner is on partnering with others to learn them. If a skill is a simple technical one like reading a balance sheet, you can send a person to a class, even online, or have the person read a book. However, for a deep-smarts skill such as figuring out how to close a complicated deal, the only way is to spend time over an extended period with someone who has mastered this skill.

Having a development partner teach deep-smarts such as how to let someone go with dignity, influence a challenging key stakeholder, or give meaningful feedback is the most enjoyable and cost-effective way to learn these tricky skills. It hands down beats the alternatives, such as investing only in classroom training or depending entirely on the manager to transfer these kinds of skills.

Guide People to Make a Good Learning Contract

EDMs know that another helpful step in getting the most learning from development partners is to structure the deal explicitly. This step is often called contracting. Don't worry: it's not about calling in the lawyers. Contracting just means making the relationship clear and acceptable to both sides. When people approach development partners, they are in effect applying to be apprentices, if only for a short time. EDMs help their employees get off to the right start by teaching them to be alert and sensitive to the demands and pressures their development partners are experiencing. Think about it: if you were being approached to be a development partner, wouldn't you want the apprentice to be flexible about time demands and offer something in return?

Let's pick up on that last point. We suggest that you help your employee go beyond basic contracting to sweeten the deal. Think about the impact of having your employee find ways to make the development partnership a mutually rewarding experience. What a pleasant deal that would be for the partner: a two-way exchange instead of being on the hook to provide all the value. For example, one person we talked to offered to reverse-mentor a development partner. This employee taught him some of the latest social networking techniques, and the development partner taught her how to approach a tough negotiation with an internal provider. There are lots of clever ways to make the relationships an exchange. Just remember to take the time to ask your people, "What are some creative ways you can reciprocate to provide value to your development partners?"

Tool Kit
A Discussion Guide to Use When Employees Plan Their Contracting

When you sit down with employees, start with this list to help them get ready to develop a robust and complete contract with their development partners.

» Have your employees describe their learning goals very specifically. Help them articulate exactly what they want to learn and why.

» Guide them to check for fit with the potential partner. Suggest that they ask, "Is this something you know about? Is this something that you are willing to help me learn?" If the answer is no on either count, advise them to ask the person to recommend possible other partners.

» Be sure to explain the benefit of crafting an approach that works for both them and the development partner. Point out the need to think ahead to consider how they will deal with time constraints and preferred ways of communicating for both parties. Explore options for watching the development partner use the skills in action or for the development partner to observe them using the skills.

» Advise them to be very open to other ideas the partner may have to help them learn.

» Remind them of the importance of agreeing on the very next steps and following up with a written action plan.

Help Make Learning Stick

"Use it or lose it." This common phrase is often used to drive home a simple but often forgotten point: learning doesn't really sink in until it is applied to real work. The good news is that learning gained through a development partner is more likely to be applied than workshop learning. It is initiated and customized by the learner and comes in natural installments that can be applied to pressing needs. In other words, it is driven by the individual seeking just the right learning needed right now to get results. She will be highly motivated to apply the learning—a real side benefit that makes your management job easier.

The bad news is that if you, as the manager, choose to be a passive bystander, the learning will not be as broad or as deep as it could be if you'd stayed involved. Even though you may have outsourced some teaching, you still play an important role by ensuring that the learning is integrated into work. Look for proof of use. If your employee has simply gained new superficial knowledge, you won't have to look all that hard. Simply watch to see if the individual uses it to get results. If so, reinforce its applicability, recognize the growth, or possibly even reshape the application as your employee uses the learning on the job. If the employee is working on a behavioral skill such as listening ability, you'll find that getting proof of use is a little trickier. For really deep smarts, like learning how to influence key stakeholders who are opposed to an initiative, you'll need to be in the picture longer, as will the development partner. You might be part of a trio for an expanded time frame. Expect to have many checkpoint discussions as your employee gradually changes assumptions and behaviors. Only over a longer arc can you, the development partner, and the individual declare victory in using deeper smarts.

Tool Kit
Ways to Extend Learning That Employees Receive from Development Partners

» **Deliver instant positive feedback.** When you see people using the new skill, call it out—especially if the use is good. But also call it out and comment if it needs adjustment. (See Chapter 1 for tips on giving useful feedback.)

» **Multiply opportunities for use.** When people have learned a skill from others, see if you can identify other assignments besides their regular jobs to give employees more chances to use the skill. For example, a lawyer learning the skill of clearly summarizing the point at the beginning, not the end, from another attorney gained additional practice when her manager assigned her to the firm's marketing task force.

» **Learn more by teaching.** When people acquire skills from others, encourage them to follow the advice "learn, use, teach." For example, Tom, who had learned how to ask great interview questions from sitting in on interviews with a peer, hosted some brown-bag lunches to teach other supervisors the art of great interview questioning.

The bottom line is that new skills are new habits. They become routine only with proper, repeated use. Even if other development partners, not you, are the source of new learning, you play an incredibly important role by helping your employees deepen, widen, and hold onto the gains through repeated use and your constant feedback.

4. Invest in a Network of Future Development Partners

Casey was a manager who attracted people who wanted to develop themselves. He had a reputation for having a ready-when-you-need-it network of development partners. Jason, who had worked for him for a year, said, "I don't know how he does it. When I need someone to help me develop, Casey has the most amazing recommendations right at his fingertips. And these people are ready and willing to help. They must owe him or something. I'm just so happy to be the beneficiary of his network."

What Casey achieved was not a mystery. It was a conscious investment. To start this amazing portfolio of ready development partners, he invested his own time by serving as a development partner for people in other departments. In a way, Jason had it right. Managers of these other departments did "owe" him. Casey explained, "When I am asked by others outside my department to help develop their staff, I get a form of social payment. I like to run up an account by investing in their staff so that I can ask those other managers to help develop mine in return."

Casey also got near-term benefits from paying it forward and being a development partner for other departments' staff. "I get to buff up my development coaching skills," he said. "I like it because I feel like I have new space that comes from being freed up from the parameters of performance demands. I seem to get a new appreciation of what really works, and I become more creative with my staff."

A second way to invest in future development resources is to get ahead of the curve by stocking up on development partners in advance, as seen in Samantha's approach.

Samantha was a manager who was a great talent scout. She actively scanned the environment to build up an inventory of development partners even before they were needed. She took great pride in her extensive database of who knew what and who were the best teachers. It included development partners her staff had used as well as people she had sought out and earmarked as potential development partners. She called it her "gold account." When we asked Samantha why she did all this extra work, she said, "Having a rich set of prequalified development partners makes matching more efficient and cuts down on the time and effort I need to invest to find the right development partners. And by the way, it helps me avoid overusing and wearing out the obvious choices."

You could take Samantha's approach one step further by swapping or combining lists with other managers. There are loads of other ways to build up your database through scanning organization charts, keeping conference agendas with presenters' names, and targeted networking, to name a few. We haven't met anyone yet who does development partner "speed dating," but who knows . . . you could be the first!

▶ Case in Point ◀

Ruth was excited and apprehensive at the same time. She had just moved from managing a staff function to a new business development function within a well-respected benefits planning and risk management firm. The shift felt huge to her. "Yikes," she thought, "they are relying on me to develop new relationships so that the sales people can turn them into clients. I've never done anything like this before."

Both Ruth and her boss, Bill, knew that reaching out to development partners was the best way that she could learn, since he also had limited business development experience. Ruth and Bill conferred and determined that although the firm was looking to build new relationships over time, Ruth wanted to hit the ground running as soon as possible. They identified the broad goal: build rapport with potential new clients and gradually help them see the benefit of doing business with the firm. Bill and Ruth agreed that the specific learning strategy would need to be a work in progress because they both lacked clarity about exactly what Ruth needed to learn.

They started by focusing on each What? and then each Who? Bill and Ruth discussed the best ways to learn from the connections, paying special attention to just how deep the learning was and how to structure the deal with each development partner.

Here's the plan they came up with and what Ruth did to implement it with Bill's support:

What? Learn how sales pros work their territory—about the variety of customers served, the profile of the ideal customer, and the customers' perceived benefits of working with the company. Learn how to close the sale.

Who? Sales pros who would be willing to have Ruth shadow some sales call.

What happened: Because some of the learning from sales pros wasn't so deep, Ruth could indeed achieve her goals with a day of shadowing. But the learning about closing deals was much deeper. Bill guided Ruth to carefully select two sales pros who were inclined to coaching others and with whom she already had good working relationships. Bill then helped her structure a deal that would respect their short time supply. They would take her on sales calls, and afterward Ruth would have very efficient debriefs, using a short list of questions.

What? Learn the components and practices of a business development job and identify the skills most important for success.

Who? Business development pros of other service organizations (not competitors).

What happened: It was a bit *harder* to identify and recruit business development learning partners who were willing and able to help Ruth learn the ropes. They were busy and focused on their own goals. Bill intervened, made some calls, and pulled in some favors to open doors for Ruth. He also coached her to break what she needed to know into smaller bite-size pieces and describe it very succinctly. This exercise helped her contract with two very good business development pros and to divide the learning needs between them. It worked. She found that the most important thing was to structure the process to work out mutually agreeable time frames. And she sweetened the deal by offering to share what she learned from her benchmarking with the business development pros.

What? Learn how the decision makers in customer organizations think about their benefit and risk management needs.

Who? CEOs and CFOs she met through professional organizations who would speak broadly about their business and how they make decisions about risk and benefits.

What happened: This one had Ruth stymied for a while. First, Ruth joined the Association of Corporate Growth, a professional organization dedicated to high-growth businesses. Its members were primarily executive members like the CEOs and CFOs she had identified as potential development partners. She feared that if she was too direct about her needs, she would scare people away. But if she held back too much, she wouldn't make an impression. She and Bill talked at length about how she might tread softly to learn how her customers perceived their businesses. This deep learning required great finesse. It would be important that these busy CEOs wouldn't think a development meeting with her was going to be a bait-and-switch to a sales call. She picked a few CEOs and CFOs who seemed natural mentors. She played it slow and cool, taking on additional leadership roles in the association that gave her a chance to naturally spend more time with the executives she had identified. Over time, this strategy paid off handsomely in terms of learning and networking.

As both she and Bill had anticipated, the learning plan evolved and challenged both of them to keep one step ahead of the demands of the job. He helped her use what she learned by asking good questions and giving good advice that helped her make sense of what she learned and how to apply it without being overwhelmed.

At the close of the first year, Ruth commented, "If it hadn't been for Bill, I would have eventually learned what I needed, but it would have taken three years." Bill summed it up this way: "It was fun to take the learning journey with Ruth. I learned along the way, too. I couldn't have been much help if I hadn't seen the role through her eyes. I enjoyed the direct coaching and teaching, but I think the biggest kick for me was seeing her learn from others." They both noted the riches Ruth received from learning from development partners. "We're sold on this approach and will continue to use it for the next round of learning," they said.

Key Points for Connecting People with Development Partners

▸▸ Give people the permission and motivation to find and use development partners who can teach them skills you don't know or don't have time to teach. Share how you have used development partners effectively in your career.

▸▸ Teach staff how to target a clear What? to learn so they can find the right Who? to help them learn it. Figure out these two "compass points" in that order and in advance, and the identification and focus of learning partnerships will be easier and more efficient.

▸▸ Help staff get the most out of learning from partners by matching the complexity of the learning with the right partner, working out a mutually satisfactory "contract," and remaining involved to ensure that the learning is processed and applied on the job.

▸▸ Continually develop an inventory of potential development partners. "Pay back" managers who provide development for your staff by being a development partner for people they send your way.

4 Teach Skills to Navigate Organization Politics

"WHICH WOULD YOU PREFER: to be right and have no one listen, or to be useful and have a fan club?"

> *Years ago, Leah's manager put that question to her. She was confident that she had the best solution for a new balanced scorecard tracking process. Even though her idea may have been cutting-edge and effective for other organizations, it simply wouldn't fly in their company. He helped Leah understand that no matter the strength of the technical solution, the process would flop without sensitivity to what would work for their company's managers. Better to modify the approach, give managers the tools that would work well for their situations, and watch the process take root and bloom, he suggested. "Seek success rather than perfection." That five-word phrase has been a very sticky lesson for her over the years; she has used it as sage guidance to address tough organization politics with skill.*

For a long time, exceptional developing employees (EDEs) have been telling us about the significance of increasing organizational political awareness and amplifying the accompanying skills. Wendy has heard this loud and clear as she helped build and lead a very successful mentoring program in the Philadelphia area for early-in-career professionals (typically in their late twenties). Year in and year out, the career-enhancing insight mentees rave about is the importance of managing organization politics. Likewise, the EDEs in our research sent the same message. Interestingly, they called out the practice of learning to navigate organizational politics more distinctly than the exceptional development managers (EDMs) we interviewed. When asked about the biggest impact their best developmental managers had on them, a large number of EDEs stated that they were taught to navigate the political terrain and what a huge difference that made for their effectiveness and recognition in the organization. They told us, "My manager expanded my thinking about the impact of culture," "He helped see what was required to truly apply my craft," and "She asked me phenomenal questions to help me understand my stakeholders and how to engage them."

In short, their best developmental managers illuminated the political landscape and sharpened their ability to traverse it— insights that were tough to learn prior coming into their roles.

In your daily interactions, have you noticed employees who diligently set out to do the right thing but then miss the mark without ever understanding why? Many, many employees need help developing political finesse.

Two colleagues we'll call Lydia and Lyndon identified a very practical solution for increasing hospital efficiency. They believed that practicality itself would make it a winning solution. But at the project meeting, they were blindsided when another seemingly lesser idea from peers got the green light instead. When they found out that their peers had talked to some of the decision makers prior to the meeting, they felt cheated. They didn't understand the importance of building confidence among key players before the decision-making meeting. Were they politically naïve? Unskilled at seeing, much less navigating, the political terrain? We'd say yes. If Lydia and Lyndon had learned how to leverage the organization dynamics, the sizable effort they had put into finding a solution would have had an altogether different outcome.

How to Teach Skills to Navigate Organization Politics

Some managers like to brag about their department's terrific analytical, marketing, or operating skills. Being great at these functional capabilities are indeed accomplishments to savor. Why don't we hear managers talking about their team's political savvy and influence skills in the same way? Let's face it: these skills aren't often acknowledged as part of your employees' job. And these skills are a whole lot less objective, less technical, less measurable—and far more difficult to teach—than functional skills. Managers find lots of reasons to short-shrift the political and influence skills. We contend that your employees' results and motivation will be greatly diminished if you do. In fact, their political missteps could end up putting you into an emergency-response mode, cleaning up organizational debris and patching the wounds of offended power players and injured employees.

One of our favorite management authorities, John Kotter, a professor at the Harvard Business School, has long guided

managers to help employees develop important influence relationships early in their careers. According to Kotter, a myopic
focus on tasks, accomplishments, and promotions can fuel your
employees' success for just so long. Their limited attention to
developing influence and relationship skills will eventually stall
their effectiveness. To have personal impact, they need the skills
that lead to smooth, responsive, and influential relationships,
even when their level of control is limited.[1]

So it's no wonder that a distinguishing approach of EDMs
is helping their employees learn practical political skills. They
call it out as a development priority as they go about making talent their business. Growing the organizational political skills of
their employees truly serves the business. With these skills well
developed, employees not only create solutions but also see them
through to adoption. They learn how to read potentially volatile
situations and know what it takes to influence positive outcomes.
Their performance improves when they are politically proactive,
know how to avoid pitfalls, and effectively influence others.

Consider This
Knowing Which Employees Need to
Develop Political Skills

How do you know if you need to step in and equip employees
to navigate the political terrain? Consider stepping in if your
employee

» Expects that logic or the sheer quality of an idea will
alone be enough to have it accepted

» Has a new role that moves him into an environment
different from the one in which he's been operating

» Receives feedback from peers or customers that her
ideas and solutions are not practical

» Indicates that others were given (or took) credit for work he completed

» Is assigned only tactical tasks by internal clients, not strategic efforts

» Has no idea how to identify key influencers in a situation

Sophisticated political skills become even more important as organizational life becomes increasingly complex every year. What's unique about teaching the "deep smarts" described in Chapter 3 is that they are capabilities that are softer, more complex and take longer to master. Though they are crucial, they are not explicit in most professions or taught to people in school. Yet what an impact these skills can have on success! Your employees can immediately use these skills and fine-tune their application for virtually all work assignments you send their way—and still keep their footing as they get on with business. Increase their political skill and multiply their impact by focusing on the following four actions:

1. Clarify and adjust assumptions about organization politics

2. Help map the bumpy political terrain

3. Coach employees to build a portfolio of politically smart approaches

4. Prepare for and sometimes rehearse the handling of politically complex situations

1. Clarify and Adjust Assumptions About Organization Politics

It's sad but true: organizational political skills often have a bad reputation because some people use them as unprincipled tactics for self-serving purposes. Organizational politics, handled poorly, can disrupt your department's flow and performance by fueling unfounded speculation, using up valuable resources, and extinguishing employees' enthusiasm. No wonder your employees prefer to tread lightly and avoid delving into anything that seems political.

Yet EDMs know that politics are an ever-present part of organizational life. According to our colleague Joel DeLuca, "political savvy" is not about acquiring power. Instead, it's about making an impact in specific situations. He suggests that political savvy has little to do with your level in the organization and much more to do with how appropriately you build support for ideas you care about.[2]

EDMs begin to unwind employees' self-limiting attitude about organizational politics by helping them examine their hidden (or partly hidden) assumptions about organization and political dynamics. Some of the common assumptions they tackle are

+ "Working in the political system is risky and will hurt my career."

+ "Using influence is self-serving and doesn't portray me as a good team player."

+ "The only proper way to operate in the organization is through the formal, hierarchical structure."

+ "Asking about the history and relationships surrounding a challenge will lead me on a wild goose chase and be a waste of time."

Of course, when handled properly and ethically, the opposite is true for each of these assumptions. In fact, the more your employees are able to read the dynamics, know others' interests, understand the informal ways the organization works, and test ideas before making proposals, the more they are able to create and sell effective solutions.

Consider this example of an EDM named Andrew who helped a staff member uncover his assumptions and increase his political awareness.

Thad, a young mechanical engineer, was responsible for reporting on the retooling of a manufacturing line. For an update meeting with Andrew, Thad armed himself with lots of statistics that would prove his case. To Thad's surprise, Andrew opened the meeting with a question: "Have you asked the plant manager where employees face the most obstacles on the line and what work conditions could be improved?" "Why would I do that?" asked Thad. "I have a solution all set up for optimal efficiency. And besides, I feel funny about speaking with the plant manager directly. It makes me look like I don't know what I'm doing or that I'm begging for his attention."

To help uncover a few of Thad's false assumptions, Andrew played out two scenarios: one in which Thad went into the presentation with his terrific efficiency solution and no prior discussions and the other in which Thad's advance work with the plant manager and talking to people on the line led to a solution more likely to be embraced by the plant personnel. Andrew talked Thad through the right approach to take with the plant manager. They brainstormed the appropriate questions. Thad would need those in addition to his great efficiency ideas. The benefits of the second scenario became crystal-clear to Thad. Andrew had given him some tools and direction. Going this route would lead to the implementation of a winning solution that truly satisfied the customer and make a much bigger impact on the plant.

Through this process, Andrew had unearthed Thad's false assumptions about talking with the plant manager. He helped Thad understand that effectively talking with him was neither risky nor self-serving. Andrew also helped Thad adjust the assumption that it wasn't important to talk with individuals on the line. Getting beyond these false assumptions and adjusting his tactics accordingly made all the difference for Thad. Being more politically adept, Thad proceeded to multiply his impact—and learn valuable lessons that he could carry forward.

2. Help Map the Bumpy Political Terrain

"If you can't see it, you can't ski it." While some Olympic skiers simply feel the terrain beneath them and turn in a winning performance, most skiers need to get a view of the slope before they can make it down the mountain at top speed. They need to anticipate the moguls and have an idea of the icy areas or other obstacles to avoid. Wendy once skied a trail in Killington, Vermont, on an incredibly foggy day and almost fell off the mountain! Not having a visual of the terrain almost doomed her. That's why the chair lift ride over a new trail is helpful to many skiers.

It's like that for many of your employees when it comes to organization politics. Because they don't have a natural feel for the way things operate, they can run into obstacles, creep to a halt, or "fall off the mountain" of organizational success. We all know there are complex dynamics wherever there are people interacting in relationships—in our families (a downright labyrinth for many of us), schools, and workplaces. What makes these dynamics difficult to discern and elusive to manage is that the operating system for those dynamics is hidden from view. EDMs give their employees a real advantage when they help their employees get up on the chair lift to see the full landscape of organizational dynamics. Then they go a step further to coach them around the danger points. Seeing the entire landscape also speeds these employees' progress because they gain perspective about how their piece fits into the bigger picture.

EDMs often work closely with their employees, sitting beside them in the chair lift to point out features of the terrain. See how Ellen did just that.

Jorge really appreciated that his boss, Ellen, had been a terrific advocate for his team, which was developing a new supply chain tracking approach that had the potential to save the company millions every year. The team members were hopeful that acceptance of the new approach would require just a few more tweaks with Ellen and then a straight line from her to final sign-off by upper management.

To their surprise, Ellen suggested what seemed to them a circuitous route as she helped them map the political terrain. Instead of going straight for acceptance, she helped them devise a threefold plan to help them map the terrain: First, understand how to satisfy clients' needs; then build stakeholder interest and buy-in for the new tracking methods; and finally, understand upper management's concerns about what it would take to implement the plan.

Ellen suggested they start by gathering information about the clients' needs. She told her team "It's really important to get a good feel for client interests, tolerance for risk, and how to meet their needs." After they spoke with a number of clients, Ellen guided them to check in with stakeholders who would also be affected by the new tracking methods. She told them, "There's an informal network of influence here, and you need to understand

*who influences whom." Ellen helped the team learn about stake-
holder influences and built what the team learned into its strategy
for winning approval.*

*Then Jorge asked Ellen to help him understand manage-
ment's concerns about implementation. He requested that
Ellen speak with upper management and test their willingness
to make trade-offs between delayed deadlines and new breakthroughs. Ellen thought this was a smart idea. Because she had
more avenues and greater credibility for influencing management, she set up the follow-up meetings but had Jorge join her
when she met with managers.*

*Ellen allowed her team to see the wider landscape by guid-
ing team members through each aspect of the mapping process.
They learned not only about client and stakeholder interests
but who was approachable and who was not, who could influence whom, and each stakeholder's bottom-line requirements.
The team members had been unaware of all the clients' and
executives' vested interests and how they might have derailed
acceptance of the new system. They were amazed at how much
political work they needed to do in order to navigate the terrain
and establish a foundation of trust with decision makers. By the
way, with this terrain map as their foundation, they later built
a strategy for winning approval. With Ellen's guidance, their
recommendation for the new supply chain tracking system got
the green light and not only saved the company considerable
money but also eased requirements placed on customers—a
double win.*

No matter the level of complexity, people will benefit greatly
by understanding who will be affected by their game plans and
in what ways. Try asking your employees to start by practicing

these political mapping skills on a small scale—for example, by using a more politically sensitive approach to getting coverage when they want to take the afternoon off.

Tool Kit
Identifying Invisible Obstacles

Where should employees be on the lookout for invisible obstacles in your organization's terrain? Start by making them sensitive to the following issues.

» Corporate culture and hidden operating rules

  Idea: Ask employees to do some detective work on what types of actions and recommendations win ready approval in this company and which are tough for management to swallow.

» How the employees' interests intersect with those of others, identifying any ripple effects the employees' suggestions might have

  Idea: Have employees work as a group at a flipchart to create a "stakeholder interests" chart. Write the employees' new suggestion in the center of the chart, and then identify all groups that will be affected and in what ways. This process might lead employees to some interesting discussions with the stakeholders that uncover invisible obstacles.

» The informal system of who influences whom

  Idea: Point out that lines of influence do not necessarily follow the organization chart. Ask employees to identify the various parties who might influence acceptance of their proposal. Have them look at the

strengths of the relationships between these players.
Have them identify who they might be able to tap to
influence others they aren't well connected with (for
example, "We need Sam's endorsement, but he doesn't
know us very well. Let's get our internal customer,
Beth, who loves this idea, to speak with him").

» The power structure surrounding a particular issue:
Who might be the supporters? Who might oppose?
What does each group want?

Idea: Have employees consider what's known about the
positions key influencers will take to the team's proposal. Support need not be unanimous, but the team
needs to know where people stand and what interests
will need to be satisfied.

» Timing and current circumstances: What's going on
right now with people who will be affected by the recommendation? How can the idea be positioned to appeal to
their interests?

Idea: Have employees research current initiatives and
pressures in the decision makers' organizations. Have
employees consider how their proposal can be advan-
tageously timed for stakeholders and possibly even
provide results that relieve other pressures stakeholders are facing.

3. Coach Employees to Build a Portfolio of Politically Smart Approaches

Mapping the terrain, though eye-opening, is just the first step
on the way to results. Employees will need to act on what they
learn. In addition to being a guide through the unfamiliar land-

scape, an EDM also serves as a coach to develop employees' political skills in three key areas: set a strategy, influence others, and adapt familiar skills to political situations.

Set a Strategy

As you saw in the case of Ellen and her team, the terrain map they drew up was just the front end of their approach. They also had to develop a solid strategy to work with influencers, customers, other stakeholders, and management to ensure viability of their recommendations.

Consider this example of how one employee, with the help of his manager, turned his knowledge of the political terrain into a strategy for influence.

> *Mitch, a medical science liaison, was asked to develop a plan to obtain buy-in from key opinion leaders for further development of a new drug. With so many potential drugs in the pipeline, endorsement of the key opinion leaders is a make-or-break step to ensure continued funding in this and other large pharmaceutical companies. After mapping the territory (finding out which key opinion leaders to tap, identifying other projects on their plates and the associated deadlines), Mitch asked his boss, Kathy, for help in creating a strategy.*
>
> *A series of discussions with Kathy provided Mitch with the help he needed to successfully influence key opinion leaders. Mitch was fascinated to learn tips for avoiding the pitfalls that would open up if he did not fully understand their major interests—tips that included:*
>
> + *Be ready with a tailored line of questions to home in on what mattered most to them and what were the "must haves."*
> + *Investigate what recommendations in the past have been viewed favorably and unfavorably and why.*

◆ *Identify and address individuals opposed to the effort and get a detailed understanding of their rationale for opposing the further development of the drug.*

    Kathy helped him understand the importance of talking with crucial influencers before presenting ideas to them at a meeting and even of asking some of them to be willing to offer their favorable ideas about the drug in question at the meeting.

    When Mitch panicked about the number of key opinion leaders who might not endorse continued development of the drug, Kathy pointed out that he didn't need 100 percent in favor. As long as he won more than half of them as endorsers, he would have the critical mass to keep the project moving forward. Mitch became determined to ensure that he had at least this level of support before his proposal came up for discussion at the meeting.

    Armed with this insight, he developed a great strategy to uncover key opinion leaders' interests and gain endorsement from the majority of them. Adjusting the strategy as discussions played out, he tailored messages to the specific players and worked through situational influence strategies.

What did Mitch learn about creating a strategy to approach a political situation within his organization? Take a look at this "Good Examples" feature, which summarizes his lessons learned and also spells out actions employees take to build their strategy.

 ## Good Examples . . .
For Guiding Employee Actions to Build a Strategy in a Political Environment

Help employees identify actions they can take to build a useful strategy in a political situation. Think about these points as potential advice to them.

» Thoughtfully sequence conversations, starting with supporters, to help build your case and get beneficial advice.

» Be ready with the proper information and precisely tailored questions that will interest key players and demonstrate your desire to fully understand their point of view.

» Research what similar recommendations key stakeholders have viewed favorably and unfavorably in the past and why.

» Identify where there could be win-wins for different key players.

» Continually build momentum from conversation to conversation among a diverse set of leaders.

» Speak with individual influencers to find their interests prior to presenting ideas at the decision-making meeting.

» Ask some endorsers to be prepared to speak up at the meeting.

» Define success not only by the results you achieve but also by how good the other influencers feel about the process.

Influence Others

Influencing others with respect and candor is a skill your employees need in order to secure their safe and successful passage through the political landscape. Because most effective employees use some form of influence skills, your role may be only to fine-tune or customize their existing capabilities. EDMs often use their day-to-day coaching time to help employees reflect on how they handled themselves in situations in which they had expected to influence others. These managers pose challenging questions to pinpoint what attracts others to their ideas or repels them—questions like "What are they likely to find in your ideas that helps them meet their objectives?" or "How might your approach disrupt their status quo?"

EDMs also teach by exposing employees to good role models. One exceptional manager shared this high-impact tactic with us: he makes it his business to expose employees to meetings with seasoned players. He asks that the employees act like anthropologists, observing the influence techniques that came naturally to these experienced colleagues.

The best influencing strategies start with a crucial examination of one's own intentions. Managers can help guide employees in checking their intentions. Sooner or later, others in the organization will be able to spot those employees who are manipulating and maneuvering for their own advantage. It is those people with negative, self-serving, or hidden intentions that give "political savvy" such a bad reputation. In the hands of an employee whose sincere intentions are to serve customers or meet important organizational goals, seeking to influence others is a positive attribute. But with the wrong intentions, the same influencing capability can be downright nasty. Think of how Star Wars's Luke Skywalker (a hero) and Darth Vader (from the Dark Side) embodied the same capabilities but used them for vastly different intentions.

Exceptional managers coach employees on how to act with integrity when influencing others. Shortcuts, white lies, and empty promises are inevitably noticed and undermine the employee's influence in the particular circumstance and in the future. Tricked clients, shortchanged coworkers, and manipulated executives never forget. When your employees use their influencing skills for personal gain, they write their own epitaph.

Influence also takes confidence. Some EDMs we spoke with instinctively knew that their employees would need to work on getting comfortable using their influence with decision makers. Feeling at ease with influence methods is a must if you expect to create meaningful change. It's a key point made by Jeffrey Pfeffer of Stanford's Graduate School of Business, a professor who specializes in the study of power. He lets his grad students know that any new plan worth implementing is controversial and that individuals and groups with counteragendas will fight it. He notes, "When push comes to shove, you need more than logic to carry the day; you need power."[3] He's right. Introducing any significant new business approach will generate controversy. And because logic alone is often insufficient, your employee had better be ready to wield considerable influence to attain buy-in.

Good Ideas . . .
For Coaching Employees to Further Develop Their Influence Skills

Most of your employees already have some influence techniques mastered; they have needed them in order to progress in the organization. When it comes to handling politically sensitive situations, they will benefit by boosting those skills and adding more to their repertoire. Winning favor for new ideas or standing their ground with a point of view is not for the ill-prepared or the fainthearted.

Have employees identify what will attract key players to their ideas and what will repel them. Be ready with a line of questioning like the following that focuses employees on the customers, stakeholders, and others (perhaps not yet identified) involved in their sphere of influence.

» Given the key individuals you want to influence, what connections can be made between your ideas and their unit's objectives?

» What can you realistically offer as an incentive (for example, your help on a project)? What are you willing to give up as a trade-off?

» What facts, figures, or endorsements will increase their interest?

» What personal or emotional appeal might your approach have (for instance, it elevates something they are passionate about)?

» How might they believe that your ideas conflict with their objectives?

» How might implementation of your approach disrupt their operations?

Also help employees examine their intentions for this round of influence. For example:

» When you dig deep, what do you really hope to achieve with this approach?

» Are you in a position to follow through on promises you make?

» Will the result be as beneficial for them as it is for you?

» Is your approach fair to everyone involved? Will anyone get hurt or feel used?

» Is everything you are suggesting in keeping with company guidelines?

Finally, have your employees identify role models to watch. Ask these questions:

» Who is particularly trustworthy and credible in their influence approaches?

» What stands out about how these credible influencers exert their influence on others?

» By contrast, are there others (no need to provide names) whom you see as misusing their influence? If so, in what ways?

Round out your coaching by jointly assessing each employee's current skills and identifying what needs to be modified or added. You will both be pleased you had the discussion. Keep the door open to ongoing dialogue as your employees apply what you have helped them learn.

Adapt Familiar Skills to Political Situations

"Putting together a plan for improving the customer experience with the joint task force doesn't really seem like my expertise, boss. Why was I selected to fill in until William gets back from leave?" We often hear questions like this from employees when they are "volunteered" for assignments that seem outside their normal scope. Take Reena, for example.

Reena was already on overload and a bit perplexed when her manager, the head of logistics at one of the largest plants of a global food company, asked for her help. He answered her question "Why me?" this way: "You're right, Reena. If I were look-

ing for our team's representative to be an expert on the customer experience, I might have picked someone with more tenure. But before William went on leave, he told me that the task force was stalemated and was looking to bring in an outside facilitator."

Reena's eyes widened. She had a passion for group facilitation. "But Reena, I don't want you to think of the task as simply managing those meetings. It goes far deeper." Rick went on to explain that he had seen Reena in action in tricky, politically sensitive situations. He reminded her of a week the previous winter when there were two heavy snowfalls. She handled frantic customers and the trucking supervisors with real poise. Reena found out what people's priorities were, quelled department arguments, got people working together, and negotiated new delivery times. "You have great questioning and listening skills, not to mention your ability to read people," he summarized.

"But Rick," she insisted, "I just consider that my job; those are just everyday skills, nothing special."

Rick told her, "Not everyone can do that, Reena. You are developing a terrific capability, and I'd like to see you apply it with this plant task force. They could use that kind of help."

With Rick's help, Reena figured out how to redeploy what she considered her "everyday skills" and turn them into strong assets for handling politically sensitive situations. It turns out that although Reena initially thought she'd have little to contribute, she actually helped save the day using her well-developed group dynamics skills.

Use Reena's example with employees who can redeploy familiar skills for new, politically sensitive situations. A short discussion could very well help them see how skills used in previous assignments can be put to good use in dealing with the political ramifications of a current effort. Encourage them to carve out an appropriate role on the team to support their team's impact in the political environment. With your guidance, they can expand their roles and help facilitate the department's more complex interactions.

Specifically look for and call out skills that can be shaped into valuable department assets, including

+ Building trusting relationships
+ Helping people collaborate
+ Demonstrating respect for others, independent of point of view
+ Active listening
+ In-depth questioning
+ Identifying other people's reactions
+ Clarifying priorities
+ Summarizing complex conversations

4. Prepare For and Sometimes Rehearse the Handling of Complex Situations

"I've been practicing my presentation, but I know I'm still not ready." When an EDM hears words like these from an employee who is about to appear before an organizational firing line, the EDM knows it's time for a rehearsal. Trial lawyers hire people to listen and react to their closing arguments. Top executives use expert consultants to help them prepare for interviews with the media. The U.S. Air Force would never send a rookie pilot into the skies after simply studying the manual and passing the written exam. They would put the upcoming pilot through the flight simulator a great many times before entrusting the new-comer with a real plane.

All these professionals know that rehearsing is a great way to prepare fully for big moments. EDMs take a similar approach when their staff members need to sell an idea or accomplish work in an environment that is uncertain or layered with multiple agendas. They know that taking the time to help employees prepare for and sometimes rehearse the handling of anticipated complex interactions pays off big time. So gather up a colleague or two and actually "simulate" the likely interactions the employee might face during that upcoming challenging meeting. Ensure that the employee receives candid feedback afterward. Your employee will do better after having had the opportunity to practice handling questions, listen to opposing views, think through their reactions, fine-tune messages, and adapt an appropriate personal presence.

Let's see how practicing works in real time for Sara:

As luck would have it, Donna had a mandatory meeting with a federal agency on a day she absolutely needed to go before the management committee to gain endorsement for critical and somewhat controversial recommendations from an environmental study. In a rather uncomfortable move, she handed off the environmental study recommendations team presentation to Sara. For five months, Sara had been Donna's right-hand helper and had spoken at the meetings, but now she would be the star player taking the proposal forward. She needed to ramp up quickly.

"Sara," Donna told her, "before you talk to the group, you need to know everyone's hot buttons, how you will react, and what kinds of responses you can offer. Ask your colleagues for

their ideas about how the key players make decisions. Feel free to get mine. Consider having your colleagues role-play people they know well to give you a chance to gauge how they will respond. Do not get blindsided. When you feel prepped for those meetings, come in and see me. I want to do a dry run with you. Getting these recommendations through the committee this month is really important to us. I know you can do this, Sara."

Sara showed up to see Donna in the conference room for the dry run. To her surprise, three other team members were there as well. Suddenly, it felt like the stakes were a lot higher. Sara could feel a queasiness in her stomach, and her mouth went dry. By the time Donna set the stage for the presentation, Sara had calmed herself and went for it. She gave an enthusiastic presentation, handling questions along the way. She was feeling pretty good and even cracked a joke, but her colleagues were not smiling. Instead they grilled her for another fifteen minutes. They threw in some tough questions for which Sara had no answers. By the time it was all over, Sara was ready to bolt, but Donna asked Sara into her office for a one-on-one debrief.

"You looked pretty scared at first," Donna said, "but you handled most of it really well, despite the tough questions at the end." Donna asked for Sara's views about the rehearsal and used Sara's comments as jumping-off points to provide more detailed feedback. Donna was satisfied that the rehearsal broadened Sara's perspective on the varied views and underscored what areas needed bolstering. Just as important, this practice session greatly helped Sara read her own reactions and manage her emotions. In the end, both the rehearsal and Donna's debrief sharpened Sara's attention to what was needed. Good for Donna. The preparation got accomplished, and Sara got developed. Next time Donna won't have to worry about handing over the reins.

Time-consuming? Yes. Worthwhile? Absolutely. Rehearsals yield high-value results; they are "sticky" memorable events that put employees into the simulator so that they gain a wide perspective on the external world around them as well as their own internal workings. When the stakes are high and employees have not had this type of development before, EDMs set aside at least an hour or two for this valuable development opportunity.

Tool Kit
Helping Your Employees Practice, Practice, Practice

You've heard that in real estate, it's all about "location, location, location." When it comes to preparing for potentially complex situations, think "practice, practice, practice." After helping your employees map the territory and think through a strategy, have them do a "walk-through" or actual role-played rehearsal with you or a seasoned colleague. As they undertake this practice, guide them to:

» Visualize the upcoming circumstances. Suggest that they bring to mind the other players, the positions they might take, and the questions that are likely to come up, such as "Describe to me who will be in the room and what you think they hope to see as an outcome."

» Test out the actual words and visual aids they will use in explaining their point of view. For example, ask, "How *exactly* are you going to explain the advantages of your recommendation? What's your three-minute elevator pitch?"

» Feel their own emotional response to the words they are rehearsing or the reactions they invoke. Ask them to consider how they will manage those emotions. A good question would be, "How will you manage yourself if Turner starts with his sarcastic remarks or if Johnson starts talking about his favorite approach instead?"

» Consider how they will handle tough questions or a turn in the direction of the discussion. Try "What do you think will be the toughest questions and objections? How will you handle those?"

» Build confidence about delivering their position. Hesitancy on their part opens up space for others to disagree with their proposals. Ask, "What was the turning point for you, when you realized this was the best approach? How can you bottle that resolve and take it into the meeting?"

» Identify and strengthen their personal presence in terms of voice, posture, and so forth. Several days before the presentation, ask, "What do you have in your wardrobe that comes closest to how your audience will be dressed? A power suit? A nice shirt or blouse?"

Remember to give meaningful feedback in the debrief of the rehearsal. We know managers who have even video-taped rehearsals so employees can see themselves in action. Such recordings give you evidence to address issues and, even more important, acknowledge what the presenters did well. In so doing, you will help them build their confidence before showtime.

After the session with you, your employees will have the opportunity to make changes, practice the tricky parts, and smooth out their performance. They'll feel better, and so will you.

▶ Case in Point ◀

By default and to his great surprise, Steve, was asked to lead a change effort to take eight finance departments out of separate business units and centralize them into one shared function. This organization development professional felt unprepared to face the myriad political issues that he sensed looming. A very anxious Steve immediately tapped his manager, Linda, for support, saying, "I think I'm entering a dark swamp with lots of alligators right below the surface just ready to take a bite of me."

Linda immediately picked up on the worry in Steve's voice. She agreed that these were dangerous waters. She recognized the complexity of the multilayered dynamics involved in centralizing eight independent units, and luckily, she was quite sensitive to the power plays. Linda wisely helped Steve identify an early hot-button issue: the need to shape the staffing decision process so that there would be minimal fallout among supervisors and employees. Shaping the decision process could be a point of leverage for Steve and a way for him to build credibility early on. Linda knew that Steve could deploy his current skills to help managers assess the talent, identify a proper role fit for each person, and provide employees with the resources to ensure a smooth transition.

In a sixty-minute brainstorming session, Linda and Steve further focused his game plan. They jointly set these priorities:

- Grasp the organization (and personal) objectives of the new financial executive team.

- Identify potential land mines among the supervisors and professionals being moved.

- Understand the subcultures of each of the eight units and where each group would most need to adapt in order to merge effectively.

- Anticipate how company policy could be used and perhaps flexed to align these teams on compensation and processes.

Linda and Steve set up weekly meetings to help Steve deftly map the treacherous waters, identify preferred methods for gathering data on managerial priorities, design the complex sequencing for influencing people, rehearse what would be presented at the financial department planning meetings, and anticipate challenges that would be raised. These meetings became steady and reliable testing grounds for approaches Steve would take. In a short amount of time, the meetings allowed Steve to overcome his early anxiety, increase his confidence, and gain real power and influence over the process.

Not surprisingly, after a power-packed and intensive year, Steve was recognized as a key force in making the organization changes a success. What's more, he developed a strong set of influencing skills for future use. And because of Linda's attention and his own commitment to preparation, not once did he get bitten by the alligators.

Key Points for Teaching Skills to Navigate Organization Politics

▸▸ Start by helping your employees identify and adjust their own assumptions about organization politics. Make employees acutely aware that avoiding or ignoring political dynamics will eventually undermine their contributions and is likely to produce results that are either not a fit for the environment or not well supported by others.

▸▸ Make the invisible aspects of organizational dynamics appear visible for employees by helping them get a full view of the bumpy political terrain.

▸▸ Teach employees a portfolio of skills to help them navigate the political terrain. Specifically, guide them to set a strategy, influence others, and adapt familiar interpersonal skills to politically complex circumstances.

▸▸ Use deep preparation with feedback when employees are facing complex political situations. They will do better after having had the opportunity to fine-tune messages, practice handling questions, listen to opposing views, think through their reactions, and adapt an appropriate personal presence.

chapter 5 Shape Your Environment to Drive Development

JEANNIE'S ALL-TIME CAREER HIGH was working for Lou Gerstner at American Express as senior vice-president of human resources. When Gerstner became the new group head of Travel Related Services, he promptly announced that one of his two top priorities would be developing leaders. Were people skeptical? You bet! After all, Jeannie's colleagues' experience matched the research showing that the number one reason leadership development falls flat is that many leaders don't really believe in it. In their heart of hearts, these leaders held a Darwinian view that the fittest survive and do so on their own.[1]

Clearly, Lou was a different breed of leader. He wanted a simple, direct development process, and Jeannie partnered with him to build one. But the process itself played only a minor role. The major force that led to success was the environment he created that drove development. And by the way, that environment endures today at American Express. It has spawned many generations of good leaders whose ranks include the current CEO, Ken Chenault. We hear that Ken continues to keep in peak

119

condition the leadership development environment in which he grew up.

So what did Lou do to shape the environment so effectively? He clearly and continually articulated why people development was a priority and underscored his principles—which included attention to all leaders, not just high potentials. Importantly, he went far beyond talk to action. Lots of it. He spent considerable time in division presidents' meetings—in retrospect, more time than on any other issue—discussing leaders and how to develop them. When he realized the corporate culture was not conducive to talking openly about leaders' weaknesses as well as their strengths, he shaped a safer environment by talking about his own weaknesses. When he saw that the prevailing culture encouraged divisions to hoard talent, he used arm twisting, if needed, to keep talent flowing across the organization. Lou was learning an important lesson that would be even more important during his days at IBM when he led an astonishing turnaround of the giant company: culture could eat strategy for lunch.[2] In fact, most of the discussions he and Jeannie had about the leadership development work centered around reshaping the culture. To bring about change, he used both the classic tools of reward, recognition, making direct demands, and modeling the new behaviors, as well as others Lou and Jeannie invented as they went along.

So far in this book, we've laid out four practices that ignite the spark that makes talent your business. This last practice "raises the heat" to keep the development fires burning brightly. The first four practices directed your view to individuals and teams. In this chapter, we invite you to raise your viewpoint to the level of your whole organization. Here we'll show you how to tune up your work environment to be an unending source of high-quality, deep development.

We'll give you lots of insights and practical tactics we learned from exceptional development managers (EDMs) to perpetuate the right environment even if you find that aspects of your broader organization are development-unfriendly.

What if the organizational environment outside your department does seem to be one that fights against you and your development-focused values? Approaches to address this are just ahead. The EDMs we studied shared some practical ways they deal with this issue. To be honest, we were a bit surprised by just how many of them found the need to not only work inside their immediate environment but also outside it to keep their development-supportive environment healthy. They consciously tend the borders between their world and the larger organization to make sure that forces don't inadvertently act as organizational viruses that undermine their development efforts.

Ironically, while their interaction with the broader organization may start as a defensive strategy to keep bad influences out, the interplay often ends up improving the overall environment. You, too, have a good chance of improving the whole company's talent management results—without taking career-threatening chances. You may be surprised to see just how much positive impact you can have while expanding the space for the development of your own people.

How to Shape Your Environment to Drive Development

Like Lou Gerstner, the EDMs we interviewed keenly shaped their organizations' environments to support making talent their business. Keep in mind these were middle and front-line managers as well as heads of small companies and divisions of larger companies—not the CEOs of huge corporations or institutions. What they all had in common was that they wove development into the very texture of their organizations, whether a team of five or a division of five hundred. How did they do it? Not through grand, sweeping gestures. Some was accomplished by what they said, but most resulted from their leadership actions. It was the repetition and accumulation of small actions that strengthened the developmental texture of their organizations and had a constant positive force field effect on employees.

Just as we can all pick up pretty quickly whether a particular work environment is slow and cautious or fast and risk-taking, we can sense if it is one where people continually stretch and learn or one where employees keep their noses narrowly focused to the grindstone. Exceptional development managers (EDMs) go over and above the first four practices to weave in the threads that give their environments a pronounced developmental texture. The approaches they use are these:

1. Create development abundance.

2. Shine a light on learning—yours and theirs.

3. Manage the interface with the broader organization.

1. Create Development Abundance

"Abundance." We love the democracy, the generosity, and the inherent optimism of the concept. We were delighted to find it as the big idea in Dave and Wendy Ulrich's book *The Why of Work: How Great Leaders Build Abundant Organizations That Win*. As they point out, "Abundance implies plenty: enough and to spare, fullness that overflows. If we focus attention on what we stand to gain . . . , abundance thinking can replace deficit thinking even when deficits are the rule of the day."[3] Their perspective got us thinking about how EDMs come from a place of abundance when it comes to development. Here are several ways you, too, can create development abundance.

Adopt an "Enough for All" Mentality

EDMs view development of potential as something they offer to everybody, not just people tagged as high potentials. In many organizations, the environment is sharply divided between high potentials and everyone else, and managers like you know it. Worse yet, the people in the "everyone else" category know it, too. While high potentials often get targeted training, access to senior management, added assessments, and career paths that are discussed at succession planning meetings, the "everyone elses" are left to fend for themselves. Such approaches are good for high potentials, but if talent development stops there, the company is handicapping its own potential and growth. By default, so is your department.

We learned that EDMs are remarkable in that they are very "democratic" in their attention to development. For them, the roster is not sharply divided into an "A" team of high potentials and a "B" team of everyone else. Like you, they rarely have all "A" players, and they sensibly know that their departmental results are only as strong as the whole team's skills and motivation. By taking an approach that invests in everyone's development, they create an environment of development abundance in place of one pitted with empty pockets of development.

The positive impact of abundant development on retention and engagement is clear and well documented. Our colleagues Bev Kaye and Sharon Jordan-Evans, coauthors of the definitive guide to engagement and retention strategies *Love 'Em or Lose 'Em*, find that in the surveys they reviewed, the top two reasons people stayed were exciting work and challenge and career growth, learning, and development.[4] Consider also that HR Solutions, a firm that specializes in employee engagement surveys and consulting, found that 50 percent of employees say yes in reply to the question "Have you thought of resigning in the past six months?".[5] In organizations with an abundant development-for-all mentality, employees would be more likely to answer, "No, we won't go!" because the developmentally rich environment provides strong reasons to stay.

Grow an Abundant Departmental Supply of Development Challenges

Are you worried that you might run out of development opportunities to spread around to everyone? We noticed that one way EDMs dealt with this challenge is to increase the departments' supply of learning challenges. We can almost hear you saying, "The last thing I need is a bigger workload." Hear us out. The EDM approach is to take on new challenges selectively. EDMs choose new projects that provide the best fuel for learning. By providing some stretch for the department as a whole, they keep stoking the development furnace. The heat generated warms the overall learning environment. See these "Good Examples" to examine some work that feeds the fire.

 Good Examples . . .
Of Added Work That Increases
Development Opportunities

Win friends in your organization and create development
opportunities by volunteering your department to take
on new responsibilities or projects. Handpick the work
that will give your employees the development they need.

Consider these examples:

Andrea, a middle-level manager in a logistics planning department, offered to try out a new system and help IT develop the training to implement it on a wider scale This decision enabled her to put together a development-rich project team and staff it with several people who would learn a lot from the experience.

Sid, a project leader in product development, talked with his team about taking on a particularly broken project on a tight deadline. The team members agreed to tackle it because of the learning value. They were particularly interested in further developing resilience under pressure and increasing abilities to deal with distraught clients.

Jia Li, a front-line manager in a call center, agreed to take on a project, in collaboration with the marketing department, to rewrite the scripts for handling customer complaints. This work gave his team leaders a chance to develop writing, project planning, and other important skills they wanted to learn. Because he believed they had the best ideas to do this work, this assignment would also lead to better scripts they would be proud of and feel ownership for.

You'll be pleasantly surprised at the new energy people display when you add some projects that extend your team's collective frontier. And by the way, if you develop a reputation for being willing to take on extra work to keep a sharp development edge for your staff (without overextending them), over time you'll not only get your pick of development-packed projects but also your pick of development-focused employees. Your department will be a magnet for people who want to learn and grow.

Shift Work Around to Refresh Development Abundance for All

We noticed that EDMs have cracked the code for orchestrating the work of the whole department in order to enrich everyone's jobs with ongoing development. They get up in the helicopter and look at the total workload to find creative ways to shift it around and balance it for optimal collective learning.

We first started thinking about this practical approach for making work developmental many years ago. We were reinforced in our view by this great little example in Lombardo and Eichinger's book *The Leadership Machine*. A group of supervisors met to tackle the issue of developing staff. In a plant location with low turnover. They were stymied about how they could possibly make room for development. To break the logjam, they took a "bigger-picture" snapshot of the work. The supervisors flipcharted major tasks, starred the ones that were toughest, and listed which they did, which were done by a team, and which were done by an individual. They found that supervisors themselves did many of the toughest, and one to two others did what was left. Most were in a "do this, please" role. The better way was revealed—rethink the work. They challenged themselves, asking questions such as "What could supervisors hand off that would be developmental to individuals or teams?" and "What is some important new work that is not getting done?" Their goal: make 20 percent of jobs developmental. They moved tasks around, and it worked.[6]

Consider also this example of how Destiny, a manager of an accounts payable department in a nonprofit, moved work around to reinforce an environment that drives development:

> *Destiny noticed that Ana had thoroughly mastered the task of creating work schedules for the group. Destiny thought, "There's*

*got to be a better way to keep people engaged and growing. I
don't want my department getting stale." She also saw clearly
that Danny needed to improve his ability to think through
a plan over the medium and long term. Destiny, who loved
baseball and never missed an Angels game, explained a plan
to Ana and Danny this way: "Ana, I want you to pitch some
of your work to Danny. I'm talking about the work scheduling.
Danny, we've talked about your interest in improving your
planning skills. Here's your chance. I want you to catch the
scheduling work from Ana. She'll show you how to do it and be
available to answer your questions. Ana, I have some ideas for
a new task you can pick up. Let's meet later this afternoon to
talk about it."*

By taking approaches similar to Destiny's, you'll be constantly recycling work—moving work that is no longer a challenge for people to those who can learn from it. Instead of
operating from scarcity (no new budget for training, no turnover, no new jobs), you'll be operating from abundance. This is a
strategy bound to have a positive impact on your development-
rich environment.

Check the Abundance of Your Development Actions

EDMs aggressively drive up the number of development actions
to create a dense web of learning that captures everyone in the
department.

When we say "development actions," we're talking about
things you do that cause people to develop—not things you
merely talk about. Actions really do speak louder than words.
When we asked exceptional developing employees (EDEs)
about managers who contributed the most to their development, we were given a litany of very specific behaviors and

interactions—not references to speeches or memos. It was the sheer density of development-focused interactions with their manager—a lot of them happening all at the same time—that created a deeply felt developmental environment.

Increasing the density of development actions comes not from big, dramatic acts but instead from lots of little things done often. Examples of these little things include many of the suggestions we've already made, such as

+ Asking development-focused questions at staff meetings

+ Insisting on learning debriefs at the end of projects

+ Having folks transfer learning at regular meetings

+ Acknowledging and praising team members not just for what they did but also for what they learned

+ Taking work away from a person who finds it boring and giving it to another who will learn from it and find it appealing

+ Creating learning mini-events such as brown-bag lunches or short presentations by experts

Isn't it great that to shape a powerful development environment, you can count on these and other simple acts that are in your path rather than having to plan and execute big, complex events or projects?

Can you imagine yourself taking these types of actions? Of course you can—because it's likely that you already do. The question for you is: Are you taking enough of these actions often enough to make development a regular part of the environment? The mini-assessment in the "Tool Kit" will help you determine how well you're doing in this area.

Tool Kit
Do Your Actions Stack Up?

Are you undertaking enough developmental actions often enough to weave development into your environment? Reflect on these questions. Consider discussing them with your staff. They will help you understand where you have more work to do.

» How often do I personally engage in development activities myself (the "little things" mentioned in the text, such as asking development-focused questions at staff meetings, insisting on learning debriefs, shifting work around to give it to people who will learn new skills by doing it, and so on)—daily, weekly, monthly?

» How often are my staff engaged in developmental activities?

» How many of my staff are engaged in development activities—10 percent, 50 percent, 80 percent, 100 percent?

» Are there any pockets in my organization that are low on development activities? Why is that?

» Are there any pockets in my organization that "rock" with development? Why is that?

» Do development activities feel like a routine part of the way my department operates? In other words, are they expected by employees or viewed as out of the ordinary?

» If a new hire asked other employees, "Is employee development important here?" what would people say?

2. Shine a Light on Learning—
Yours and Theirs

While the importance of true action can't be underestimated, it's also important to talk about the development you experience going on around you. Smart communication enhances an environment that is development-supporting. What works best is to shine a light on development successes or issues when or just after they happen instead of waiting. This illuminates fresh evidence.

Shine a Light on Yourself

Start by shining a light on yourself. We noticed that EDMs are fairly transparent about their own learning. Of course, they don't present themselves as dummies who never know what to do or lack skills and good judgment. But like you, EDMs don't know everything and don't make the right decision 100 percent of the time. As long as you continue to learn, you have stories you can share with your people as they unfold. Announce what you need to learn, and share your progress in learning it. That way you publicly signal your personal accountability for development.

Share the emotions and frustrations associated with learning, not just the content of what you are learning. If you make a mistake along the way, talk about it. Debrief your decisions that go awry. When you help people see how you made a decision, where your assumptions were off base, and what you learned from your mistake, you help establish an environment in which people can be honest about their mistakes and learn from them. If you never mention your mistakes, you unwittingly shape an environment where mistakes become taboo and rich learning opportunities are wasted.

Shine a Light on Your Employees

It's common wisdom that shaping an environment depends a lot on what managers model and the extent to which they hold others accountable for behaviors that they wish to make a natural part of the scene. EDMs were strong on both counts.

It may come more easily for you to shine a light on your employees' learning than on your own. That's because as managers, we're used to examining and observing people who report to us. Just as you hold people accountable for delivering business results, you need to be consistent in holding people truly accountable for learning. When talent is your business, your staff need to know you mean business when you ask them to develop beyond day-to-day requirements.

When people don't learn the skills and behaviors that you together have put into the plan, their shortfall casts a dark shadow on the environment for development. It tells others that you aren't serious about elevating learning to the same level as business results. Are you prepared, as Jack Welch was at GE, to let people go who get results but do not learn and use the behaviors that are required—even after they get feedback and have been coached? We didn't collect data about EDMs' firing rates. We do know, however, that they are willing to confront people who fail to develop expected behaviors. They aren't out to "catch" people failing. Rather they use the tactics and approaches outlined in this book to help people succeed in learning.

Of course, the other side of the shine-a-light coin is pointing attention to people's learning accomplishments. EDMs publicly reinforce and reward people for development—especially when learning accompanies business results. That's the most powerful time to make a big deal of it. It really does reinforce the double finish line of results and development. However, EDMs also acknowledge people for development progress along the way to results. In fact, when they explain the value of the learning from a project that didn't achieve the expected business results, they communicate that development really does matter.

Here's how Margie, a regional director of seven store managers in a growing retail chain, artfully shone a light on development.

> Margie was proud of Sharita, manager of one of the newer stores in a fast-growing retail footwear chain selling shoes made from recycled materials. Sharita had surmounted all kinds of challenges to staff the store, assemble the merchandise, and promote the opening. She had previously managed a restaurant, so she was on a fast learning curve to learn the footwear business. She had also made excellent use of a key player in marketing, relying on him as a powerful development partner.
>
> Without embarrassing Sharita, who doesn't particularly like the limelight, Margie worked out a way for Sharita to share her own marketing and promotion learning experience at a staff meeting to help other store managers understand that they, too, could use a similar development technique.

There are many ways to shine a light on development. Just remember how powerful it is to continually send the messages that you mean business when it comes to development. That way you dramatically improve the chances that you will in fact make talent your business.

3. Manage the Interface with the Broader Organization

So far we've focused on the inside-your-department work you need to do to create an environment that drives development.

Now we turn to the work you do outside your department to realistically protect what you create or perhaps expand what you've created. As we mentioned earlier, EDMs take challenges with the broader organization quite seriously. In this section we will explore the one that EDMs felt most strongly about: dealing with the risk aversion that frequently comes with an overemphasis on short-term results. We'll also show you how to transform organization-supplied development tools into customized gold mines for your environment.

Managing Risk Aversion

If you were a fighter pilot in wartime, would you fly above or below the radar? A war hero we know was a navigator during World War II and the Korean War, well before computers replaced human navigators. When the danger was minimal, he flew at a normal altitude. But when danger was near, he flew just above the tree line in order to avoid the enemy's radar. His daring decision worked. He survived more than seventy missions under fire and went on to have a rewarding career in business.

Organizationally speaking, sometimes the better strategy is to fly below the radar to avoid being shot down. EDMs we studied did just that. They revealed how adept they are at anticipating and dealing with their organizations' cultural bias to avoid risk, a predisposition that often translates to limited courage for fostering development. As one manager stated, "We have an action addiction in our company, and doing things like coaching or giving people development assignments is viewed as getting off track."

EDMs assess the political atmosphere as they decide whether to fly below or within the radar. Sometimes the EDMs recognize they are taking some risks to invest in development but are willing to take those chances. They simply make sure that business results remain on target. Achieving set business objectives shields their departments from too much risk-limiting scrutiny. For example, one manager said, "When my boss fussed about one of my staff, Perry, who he felt was not ready to do a sales job I put him in and wanted him fired, I held my ground, knowing that Perry would deliver. And he did. I've seen other managers give in to this kind of pressure, which leads to a waste of talent." In this case, the EDM's open bet paid off. In other cases, managers take a chance and pay the price. One manager said, "My staff have no idea how bloodied I get standing up for their development." In such situations, brave managers assess that the rewards are greater than the pain.

At other times, EDMs clear the air for a development action by registering a full flight plan with their management. Think of this as a smart way to "sell up" a development move or job extension in context. EDMs discuss a reasonable assessment of risk with their managers and explain how they will hedge the risk. This is a good way to get out in front of the natural tendency for those higher in the organization to avoid development risk. You can "sell up" a development assignment in context, making the whole picture clear. Check out the "Good Example" feature below to learn how one manager used such an approach.

 ## Good Example . . .
Of Selling Up a Developmental Move

The issue: Anthony, who runs a retail banking region, needs to convince his manager to let him move a finance officer, Thomas, into a marketing job at a time when marketing is mission critical to the region's business results.

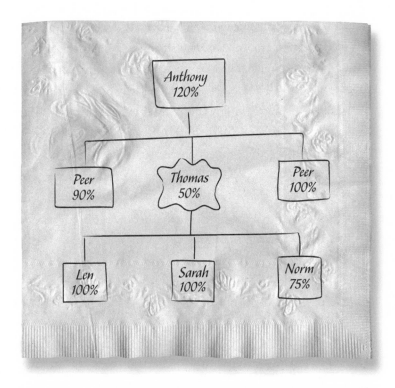

The approach: Anthony will help his manager see the move in context so that she will realize that the risk of implementing his idea is acceptable. He will explain the tactics he intends to take to manage the risk of entrusting Thomas with the marketing effort.

He uses a simple visual tool that he sketches on the back of a napkin at lunch:

Anthony makes the following points about the diagram which shows the relative marketing expertise key players.

» With his own marketing background, Anthony personally has 120 percent of the skills needed to stay on top of marketing challenges.

» Although Thomas (the 50 percent skill box) has much to learn, he can draw on Anthony and two people who will be Thomas' direct reports, Len and Sara, who are very experienced with 100 percent marketing expertise. Len and Sara stand ready to mentor a new manager and quite enjoy sharing what they know.

» Anthony reports that Thomas is a good learner. He's seen Thomas develop rapidly in other stretch assignments. Anthony assures his manager that he will commit to spending ample time to coach Thomas.

Notice how Anthony makes sure that his manager knows that the risk involved of moving Thomas is quite manageable and will not impair the marketing results his manager is concerned about.

The result: Anthony's manager is now convinced that the developmental value outweighs the risk and gives him a green light for the developmental move.

Your challenge is to not only show the development assignment in context but also to accept the responsibility to manage the risk of stretch development. Keep in mind risk reduction tactics such as

+ Providing safety nets

+ Stepping in where needed

+ Adjusting the degree of stretch

+ Using developmental partners

There's no way to have an environment that drives development without taking a fair number of chances on people. Adopt the thinking and approaches in this section, and you'll overcome risk intolerance in your organization so that you can take more chances within your department.

Get More Value out of Organization-Supplied Development Tools

Ever been stuck with a home improvement challenge and not have the right tool? Like the time you tried to hammer in a nail with the back end of a screwdriver? We all need to use the right tool at the right time for the right job. People who teach home improvement "hammer" this home.

Have you ever felt like you have been on the receiving end of a wrong-tool-at-the wrong-time in a people development situation? For example, it's "360 season" (360-degree feedback is the tool that gathers structured feedback from all directions, up, down, and sideways), and your newest employee is expected to have a 360-degree process, even though he's been in the company for only four months. Or you're required to fill in a specific development plan form that doesn't allow for the plan you already have in place for a staff member. Or you're instructed to send all your employees to a class on the latest calendaring tool even though most of your customer service team doesn't attend meetings or use calendars at all.

The 360 degree feedback process, development plan structures, technology training—these are all potentially wonderful tools. But sometimes there are simply too many of them, and none of them feel quite right for you now that you're engaging in daily development tucked into the work itself. At times like these, remember that your HR and training and development departments are trying to do their jobs well, and so are you. There are more opportunities than you might think to collaborate with the people supplying training and tools so that you are using them with the right people at the right time.

When you feel faced with a barrage of company-required development processes, you have a choice. You can dig in your heels, refuse point blank to cooperate, and earn a reputation as someone who's "not with the program" or "doesn't care about developing staff." Or you can follow the example of some politically astute EDMs in our study. These managers were quite creative about the use of tools and ultimately found ways to use them smartly as a support rather than as an interruption of their development-driving environment. It's as if the EDMs have embraced the motto "No good tool should go unused." Instead of seeing tools as problems, they see them as a sign of support that simply needs to be used the right way.

Table 5.1 provides some clever approaches suggested by EDMs that you can use to increase the value of organization-supplied tools. Tools and processes designed by the organization all have value and are of benefit to the company. HR professionals are trying their best to develop an integrated talent management system. But integration is complicated at the manager level. Here integration is about fitting parts of the system to day-to-day operating needs of the department and varying needs of individuals. Believe us, the HR professionals don't want you to simply go through the motions; most of these tools and processes actually require some tweaking by the manager to provide their greatest benefit. Make this a win-win for all by ensuring that the tools and processes are particularly

Table 5.1 ■ Tailoring Organizationally Supplied Tools to Increase Their Value to You

If the company gives you . . .	Increase its value by . . .
Performance plans that add on development targets	"Inserting" the development targets right into the "results" areas of performance plans, if not in the forms *per se*, and then in conversations with people. Sometimes EDMs use this part of the form to summarize the key actions they have agreed to. (Read more about this in Chapter 1.)
A required 360-degree feedback instrument	Taking the time to help people make sense of the feedback and focus on the behaviors they are improving to get better results. In other words, help them use the data to both refine their development goals and point the way to what they next need to develop.
A mandated number of classroom training hours per year	Negotiating for space in classes that match needs in people's development plans. If you send these people, they will already be highly motivated to use what they learn, and you won't have to spend a lot of time convincing them to go. Involve people in determining how best to apply tools picked up in training classes. Make it a must to talk about that application after class.
A form to provide input about possible successors for your role	Using the time and effort to think through and implement the stretch work that will more quickly qualify potential successors to assume your job.
	Articulating what is most important in your role and assessing potential successors against these criteria so that you can give them clear development objectives.

relevant and useful, more assets than distractions. That way, they unleash their true value.

In making your case for tailoring, take the time and use politically astute approaches to negotiate with the powers that be. Here are some examples of how EDMs have made their case and been successful in leveraging the use of tools and training.

> *Marsha is making the case with her manager, John, to send an employee to training later than currently booked. She thinks it will be more relevant for the employee in question at a later date. "John, I do not want to send Robbie to the new course on coaching. The timing is not right. Robbie is a brand-new manager. He first needs to learn how to delegate work and hold people accountable before he learns to coach. I want to send him to the coaching course, or one like it, in nine to twelve months. Can I have your support on this?"*

> *Michael is speaking with Patrick in HR. "Patrick, Betsy isn't up for a 360 now. She's still grieving the loss of her husband, and I think it's unfair to have this kind of deep, personal feedback right now. It would only upset her and not lead to any constructive change. Give me a couple of weeks to see how she gets on, and I'll come back to you to set it up. Can we make this work?"*

> *Katherine is getting her manager's buy-in to switching out participants for a training class. "Don is scheduled to take a delegation class. I bet it's because he has been identified as a high potential. I need your support to substitute Ken. I just*

promoted Ken to supervisor, and this is a skill he needs to improve now. When Ken gets back, I'll have him hook up with Don, who can help Ken apply what he learns."

A Final Note About Managing the Outside

We've touched on two types of broader organization interface challenges that can cause noise in your environment: risk aversion applied to development and required tools that are hard for you to use effectively. You may encounter others. You may be facing HR plans that move people around every two or three years, before you've had time to do the development you want. Or cost-cutting measures may mean that you are so understaffed that it's particularly difficult to shift work around. Or compensation schemes may encourage behavior that is opposite to the development you're trying to instill; for instance, you may be developing team selling skills, but all compensation has to be based on individual performance.

We whole heartedly encourage you to engage the broader organization to change these or other obstacles you face. If you have a good "development business case," you have a good chance to win your point. And here's even better news: through these case-building efforts, you can be a change agent to have a positive impact on the whole organization. It's no longer just about protecting your environment, which is important, but actually becomes about improving the whole company. It is highly unlikely that the company is purposely trying to thwart you; all that's needed is alignment of processes and interests. And that, we know, can be very hard. You can be a force for better alignment! Just watch your influence soar.

▸ Case in Point ◂

Kurt, an engineering manager, was a stickler for performance results. He liked a well-ordered department. "Everything organized and under control" was his motto. But his faith in his motto was shaken. He learned the hard way that if he played everything by the book, with each person operating strictly according to his or her job description, people lost interest in their jobs—and then he lost them. A talented engineer left out of boredom, and Kurt noticed that some others on his staff seemed less engaged. Kurt's boss was complaining that the department would miss important milestones if anyone else left.

With this wake-up call, Kurt faced the fact that his environment was suffering from a development deficit. He was spurred on to talk with Maya, a manager at an entrepreneurial firm, who was in his cycling club. Kurt admired Maya and often used her as a sounding board. She told him about a technique she used to keep people fresh, challenged, and constantly developing. She called it "work cycling," a perfect metaphor for both Kurt and Maya, given their shared passion for cycling. She described it as a technique for planning her department's work with an eye to continually shifting tasks among team members.

Kurt decided to try reassigning work. Before taking any action, he primed the department for his new focus on creating a development friendly environment. He gathered some thoughts from each of his people by asking what supported their development and what got in their way. He asked which skill each of them would be most interested in developing next. This information performed a double duty. It signaled his interest in development and gave him information he could use to construct his plan.

Being an engineer, he even found a way to use a spreadsheet to organize the assignments. Kurt stood back to think about the work allocated to his entire staff: three engineers, a quality control professional, and a production analyst.

- **Ilya, senior engineer.** Kurt had found that Ilya was interested in learning to manage. He delegated a big chunk of the on-boarding of a new engineer to him.

- **Sharon and Jonathon, engineers.** Kurt learned that they were both finding their work a little stale. Kurt decided to swap their projects, thereby giving each a new set of challenges and people to work with.

- **Marita, production analyst.** Marita was feeling bored by the grind of collecting and analyzing data every month and wanted more satisfying client interactions. She'd received feedback from clients that her presentation skills weren't up to snuff. The development solution: Kurt outsourced the data collection and mining to a staff member in the finance department. He had Marita share the data presentations for three months with another engineer who had a knack for telling the story behind the data.

- **Stephanie, quality control analyst.** Because she had already picked up some new challenges and Kurt felt that he was already dealing with a lot of changes, he decided that she would be developmentally fine for a while, just stretching to grow into her role as currently defined.

Kurt put all the moving parts on a spreadsheet so he could keep track of it. His "aha"? It was just one snapshot in time. "I'll need to look at this at least once a month and pay special attention to Stephanie's opportunity for development. I'll be on the lookout for new opportunities to allocate the work to make sure it is yielding the most development."

He also adapted the standard performance appraisal form. It was online, so he just put in a new column for development objectives in front of the results objectives. As he talked with each of his staff, they lined up the development targets against the results objectives. Kurt and the HR rep sat down to review the approach. She liked it so much that they found themselves talking about how it could be rolled out to other departments.

Kurt really did a terrific job of creating abundant development opportunities by increasing the amount and quality of development for his staff. He found ample opportunity to refashion existing work and discovered a new level of opportunity that he had not tapped. When he and Maya continued doing their 25-mile bike tours, he always had lots to share about the success of his work cycling and how it was being received.

He learned through the grapevine that Buck, his manager, was a bit concerned about too many changes in roles and the impact on the department's performance. Kurt realized he had not presented the full plan to Buck but only given him updates in pieces. His next step: lay out the whole work environment like a big flowchart to show what was changing as well as what was staying the same.

Key Points to Shape Your Environment to Drive Development

▸ Make development abundant by embracing rich develop-ment as a benefit for all employees (not just high potentials), increasing the development quotient of your department's work, and cycling tasks among people to add new develop-ment challenges. Infuse your environment with an abundant flow of development actions and routines.

▸ Shine a light on development. Share what you are learn-ing from your successes and failures, and recognize and reward good development where you see it. Also hold people accountable for development goals.

▸ Step up to managing the interface with the broader organi-zation: make sure you have the space to take some bets on development moves and assignments; always deliver results so you can cover your bets.

▸ Be smart in the use of company-provided tools and training at the right time for the right people to increase their impact.

6 Put Exceptional Development Practices into Action

BEHIND EVERY GREAT ACHIEVEMENT—especially those that bring about transformational shifts—is a dedicated champion driven to make a difference. Washington Roebling, a civil engineer who oversaw the thirteen-year-long construction of the Brooklyn Bridge, was one such champion. This structure, deemed by skeptics to be impossible, was to become the world's longest and tallest suspension bridge at the time. "In every category, it defied comparison and overawed the spectator" and was considered the greatest work since the aqueducts of the Roman Empire.[1] Completed in 1883, it became the only land link between Brooklyn, the fastest-growing city in the United States,[2] and Manhattan.

Washington's father, John Roebling, designed the bridge down to every last cable and girder and then passed the baton to his partner and son to manage the enormous (and sometimes deadly) construction project. Washington was passionately consumed by the complexities of the centenary curves, limitations of materials, cavernous bedrock, the demands of disgruntled workers, and the intricacies of cable construction.[3] Somehow he maintained the forward momentum while also addressing these huge obstacles and challenges. With the support of his wife after a crippling injury and driven by undefeatable determination, he kept plugging away, exploring and implementing new solutions.

On May 24, 1883, the hard-labored, long-awaited bridge opened to tremendous celebrations. Easy access across the imposing East River linked the cities of New York and Brooklyn to such an extent that they eventually merged into one.[4] The determination and passion of one man who refused to give up fundamentally shifted the landscape of one of the world's largest metropolitan areas.

We don't recount this story because you have a gazillion dollars and legions of staff to implement a monumental project. We tell it because making talent your business can be your lasting legacy. It is a legacy that, like the Brooklyn Bridge, may take years of determination, creativity, and passion to build. Ultimately, it will contribute to a fundamental two-layer shift in your world. It will represent both a transformation in the way you manage and a significant improvement in the results you and your team will achieve.

How to Put Exceptional Development Practices into Action

As you put exceptional development practices into action, you will find yourself in good company. Some of the most outstanding senior executives have caught on to what it truly takes to grow their businesses for the long haul: a cadre of deeply and broadly developed leaders and managers. Not only have they invested in programmatic leadership development efforts, but even more to the point of this book, they spend their *own* time coaching and mentoring the people who report to them. They also hold reporting managers accountable for doing the same thing. In leading companies such as Harley-Davidson, American Express, and Procter & Gamble, senior executives have figured out how to shift their jobs to dedicate a whopping 30 percent of their workweeks to personally developing others.[5] How can they possibly do this? It's likely that they are driven by personal values, a keen focus on the future, and an interest in achieving more through raising the capability of staff to do higher level work—all of which cement a commitment to making talent their business. As explained in *The Talent Masters: Why Smart Leaders Put People Before Numbers*, Bill Conaty and Ram Charan note that these true "talent master" CEOs believe in their heart of hearts that "Only one competency lasts. It is the ability to create a steady, self-renewing stream of leaders. Money is just a commodity. Talent supplies the edge."[6]

Like the Roeblings who spent years constructing that transformative bridge, exceptional development managers (EDMs) we spoke with crafted their people development legacy over time, often over the core years of their careers. Just as construction projects begin with plans, you begin with the guidelines in this book. Putting these ideas into action will require an investment of creativity and energy on your part. If we've done our job, you know by now that you're not going to have to work overtime to make this switch. You will, however, have to do things differently in order to enhance your results, your team's performance, and your staff's deep skill sets. As you begin to transform yourself fully into a leader who makes talent his or her business, consider the following:

1. Take your EDM practices to the next level.

2. Integrate the five practices for optimal benefit.

3. Savor the rewards.

1. Take Your EDM Practices to the Next Level

Although we've taken the shortcut of categorizing certain leaders as EDMs, the reality is that most managers are EDMs some of the time to some of their people. We assume that you, too, already use some of the approaches outlined in the book; rather than starting from scratch, you probably already have a foundation in place. So we are encouraging you to take it further by making a shift in your mind about what's most critical in your job and about how you want to be known. Once you have shifted your perspective, you can then modify your time allocation and the way you interact with others.

Your personal perspective can make a big difference in how you define your job, as illustrated by the familiar story about two workers in a large open field. From a distance, it seemed as if they were doing exactly the same thing. They both labored hard with a chisel and hammer on large pieces of stone. When each was asked what he was doing, the first worker, hunched over his workplace, did not look up when he grumbled, "I am cutting stones. Each one has to be same as the last." The second worker looked up with a pleased expression and enthusiastically responded, "I am building a cathedral." Similar to the second stonecutter, your long-term, big-picture perspective and your confidence in your skills will make a huge difference in how you view your role as an EDM and how you implement it. Let's take a closer look at both your motivation and the development of your skills.

Clarify Your Motivation for Making Talent Your Business

What motivated the EDMs we spoke with to adopt the five practices and start using them every day to pursue deep development of their staff? They acknowledged the practical business advantage of pursuing daily development: better-equipped employees, less need for re-work, increased performance, and more exciting opportunities for their teams, to name a few. Yet for many, the more fundamental driver went well beyond practicality or the boundaries of their job description. They expressed a profound belief in the value and importance of development. It infused their mind-sets and became a natural part of the ebb and flow of their work. They didn't pick up this value in a course or a book. More often their values were developed through discovery over time or learned by experiencing how their own enlightened managers developed them. One EDM told us, "Time and time again, my manager took a chance on me by risking putting me in a job I was not prepared to do. Now it's my turn to take risks on others." In some cases, when they really dug deep to think about why growing talent was so important, they told us they were ensuring their legacy—a legacy that had the potential to transform individual lives and advance their organization's performance.

How would you describe your personal motivation for taking your EDM practices to the next level? Perhaps you want to make talent your business to drive your department's performance or to respond to your employees' needs and interests or to feel the personal fulfillment that comes from being integral to others' growth. Your motivation will likely stem from more than one driver, so allow yourself a couple of minutes as you consider all the elements that make an EDM approach personally compelling to you. Making the deep link between your values and this practice will solidify your motivation, clarify your thinking, and keep you going when you face obstacles. Working from your values is more fulfilling and sustainable than simply meeting someone else's requirement of you. Your approach becomes your "way of being" instead of your task list or job description.

EDMs say they know they have made the mental shift when instead of thinking, "Why can't Matt get that project plan completed?" they think, "What can I do to get Matt fully developed in his project-planning skills?" Or instead of going home at the end of the day and sharing with their spouse the excitement of coming in under budget, they share the excitement of an employee's achievement after learning some complicated business process.

Good Ideas . . .
For Clarifying Your Motivation to Develop Others

We trust that if you have gotten this far in this book, you're a believer in developing your own EDM practice. Using the following questions, spend a few minutes to uncover your motivation. With a keen grasp of your inspiration, you will be able to rev up your energy to get started and keep going.

» Thinking back to an exceptional developmental manager who had a significant impact on you, what did you value most in his or her commitment to developing others?

» What are the long-term benefits you hope to accomplish by using an EDM approach to managing people?

» In what ways will being a more effective EDM help your career and personal life?

» What trade-offs are you willing to experience in order to invest in a long-term effort to become a more effective EDM?

» If you became wildly successful as an EDM, what would make you feel the proudest about your accomplishments?

Remember to Stretch Your Own Development Skills

Desire alone won't get you around the corner to a new way of working. As we said in the Introduction, managers all over the world have the desire but rarely the skills to make talent their business. Even the support of a resource book like this one can only be a starting point for developing new capabilities. Your path for planning and implementing a process to improve your EDM capabilities may well be similar to the one you set out for your employees. You may need to develop new "deep smarts" by working with development partners (see Chapter 3) in order to make the transformation. You'll be testing new ways of managing, building relationships, coaching, delegating, and refining your approach. We think that's pretty interesting: you may well be in your own development process, learning development from the inside out, if you will, as you simultaneously guide employees to take a similar route. Take advantage of this contagious nature of development. Instead of trying to "cure" the process (as we often do with conditions that are contagious), you'll want to spread it around and be a role model for continual learning.

Let's play with the analogy of thinking through development for your employee as a way to get ideas for how you can further your own development skills. Consider a game plan you might come up with for your employee to develop a truly complex capability. Where would you start? And what would come next? The answers may be evident from the early chapters of this book, but there is a big difference: you are self-initiating your development. Because it's often "lonely at the top," you may have limited guidance or support from your own boss. He or she may not possess daily development know-how. You may therefore have to conduct a self-assessment of your current skill capabilities and find your own opportunities to tuck development into your work. Reflect on the list of EDM skills we have provided in the "Consider This" feature below and the extent to which you demonstrate these. Not all of these skills will be of equal importance in your current situation, so determine which improved skills you need most or might make the biggest impact in your personal EDM practice.

Take it from Paul, an aspiring EDM in a large sales organization: "At first, I asked each employee to complete a development plan and talked with each one individually about their development goals. After a few months, when I saw spotty results, I decided that it was up to me to develop my own skills to develop my staff. I have geared up my listening and inquiry skills and include them in my regular way of operating with employees. I also look for daily opportunities to make every day a development day, like one-on-one's, team meetings, discussion with my HR partner, and off-site meetings. I am not stressed over not having fully mastered it yet because when I asked my employees how this is going for them, they said—with pride— that they were getting lots more development than employees in almost any other department." Just like any great life-changing habit, it will take ongoing effort, practice, reflection, and application. Paul's humility is admirable. While he knows there is always more to learn, he has taken bold steps to develop the skills he needs to help his employees grow in significant ways.

Consider This
A Sampling of Exceptional Development Manager (EDM) Skills

Rather than fill the entire chapter with the complete list of skills required of a superb EDM, we're pointing out key skills that cross the lines of the five practices. If you become keenly adept with emotional intelligence, for example, you'll be able to apply that skill to all five practices. Another skill, risk-taking, comes into play particularly for practice 1 ("Make every day a development day") and practice 5 ("Shape your environment to drive development").

We're counting on you to do some exploration and identify which of these skills, if further developed, will make the biggest impact in your current circumstances.

Broad and Long-Term Outlook

Strategic thinking: Adapting a mind-set that takes into account the broader, longer view of the business and your department's bench strength to get results

Perspective setting: Helping others understand the larger context; diminishing the drama that comes with a narrow, immediate view

Deep Interpersonal Connection

Emotional intelligence: Being self-aware and transparent; managing your own emotions and tuning in to others' interests

Discovery learning: Guiding people to discover their own lessons versus telling them what to do

Building trusting relationships: Demonstrating honesty, credibility, and caring in the relationships you build with others; doing what you say

Deliberate and Decisive Communications

Enhanced listening: Being able to read others; taking into account both people's words and the feelings behind their words

Productive inquiry: Asking tailored, thought-provoking questions that make people really reflect and discover new ways of thinking and acting

On-point articulation: Sharing sufficient detail (beyond general comments) in ways that make your message readily grasped by your employee and others; go beyond buzzwords to provide nuanced explanations in full sentences

Conviction and Character

Tenacity: Maintaining a positive attitude and forward momentum despite prevailing challenges

Risk taking: Demonstrating a willingness to move out of your comfort zone and beyond status quo; having the courage and the wisdom to take considered chances

Adaptability: Operating effectively with ambiguity or in less than ideal conditions; being willing to take the heat

Passion about development: Consistently showing a zeal for developing others and yourself

Looking at the list of complex skills can be daunting or inspiring. If you are really going to make talent your business, taking your exceptional development skills to the expert level needs to take center stage. Another way to determine where to start is to ask a trusted employee what additional actions on your part would be most beneficial in supporting his or her growth. You might be surprised by what you're told. One manager who voraciously read books to ensure he had cutting-edge knowledge was astonished to find out that the EDM attribute his employee valued most was his ability to read her and understand her.

Practice makes perfect. In addition to being a development partner for people in other departments (which paves the way for reciprocity from their managers), there is another arena for additional practice. How about being a development partner externally for nonprofits, sports teams, or even friends? We were tickled by a story from a friend coaching six-year-old girls' soccer. His experience was reminiscent of the challenge of the "curse of knowledge" that commonly afflicts individuals who want to teach others. Chip and Dan Heath talked about this issue in their book *Made to Stick: Why Some Ideas Survive and Others Die.*[7]

This curse—the difficulty of remembering what it is like *not to know* something—gets in the way of experts' attempts to develop others, particularly newbies. Our friend told us it wasn't until he coached this spirited girls' team that he really understood how to help his staff learn. He was forced to give up his "cursed knowledge" of how soccer should be played and look at it from the point of view of the players. They were more interested in fun and camaraderie than in technique and winning. He then "translated" this learning into thinking about how to develop his staff—that it was crucial to understand their interests and find a hook for their development. Think how your volunteer efforts might also give you an opportunity to hone your skills while developing those of others.

2. Integrate the Five EDM Practices for Optimal Benefit

It is commonly believed that light travels in a straight line. But light itself is a wave, so the idea that light travels in a straight line is more of a handy explanation than an exact characterization of reality.[8] The same may be said about this book. Laying out five distinct practices in successive chapters may imply that building and deploying your EDM practice is a straight-line activity. In most cases, that's not really true. A sequential pattern may actually work once in a while, but it's not the norm. We'd therefore like to set our own record "straight": though we provided these practices sequentially to help you learn them, your best use of the practices may come from combining a couple at once or even sidestepping some of the practices for a period of time. The manner in which you blend the practices for optimal impact will be determined by your unique circumstances. To help you as you consider the sequencing and combination advice here, Table 6.1 summarizes the five practices and the primary approaches associated with each one.

Combine and Sequence the Five Power Practices

What makes many of the EDMs in our study stand out is that they have mastered how to integrate the five practices in personalized and effective combinations. In effect, they customize their approach for different employees and under different business circumstances, mixing and matching the five practices to fit the circumstances.

Before we tackle customization, let's take a look at a couple of overall guidelines to follow when you plan your personal EDM practice. Always keep in mind and use practice 1 ("Make every day a development day") and practice 2 ("Tap the psychological side of development"). They provide a solid foundation for the other three, making them that much more effective. Practice 1 gives you ideas about the amount of stretch and types

Table 6.1 ■ The Five EDM Practices and the Approaches That Support Them

EDM practice	Manager approaches that support the practice
1 Make every day a development day	■ Tuck development into work ■ Create the right stretch ■ Seize development moments ■ Leverage team learning
2 Tap the psychological side of development	■ Start with yourself ■ Cultivate relationships built on trust ■ Help employees "see" themselves during key interactions ■ Connect the dots between emotions and learning
3 Connect people with development partners	■ Green-light and motivate people to partner up for development ■ Give people an accurate compass to find the right development partners ■ Teach people how to get the most learning from development partners ■ Invest in a network of future development partners
4 Teach skills to navigate the political terrain	■ Clarify and adjust assumptions about organization politics ■ Help map the bumpy political terrain ■ Coach employees to build a portfolio of politically smart approaches ■ Prepare for and sometimes rehearse the handling of complex situations
5 Shape your environment to drive development	■ Create development abundance. ■ Shine a light on learning—yours and theirs. ■ Manage the interface with the broader organization

of assignments you can provide without overtaxing employees. One EDM told us, "It took repeated attempts to calibrate the right amount of new responsibility I could give to employees. The big lesson is that each person was pretty individual as to what he or she could handle."

The second practice comes repeatedly into play because you simply can't develop people fully unless you know them as individuals and have established trusting relationships with them. You need trust in order to have employees appreciate and act on your feedback, to be a credible and welcomed source of support, and to build a connection that makes it possible for them to take the risks inherent in growth. Self-awareness—both on your part and theirs—and the motivational and engaging aspects of learning increase the impact and longevity of your developmental efforts. Although you can create some growth without self-awareness and strong engagement, these two ingredients are absolute necessities to deliver the deep development that has a lasting impact.

Take Frank's lead as an example. After discussing with his employee Louise a disappointing outcome she had in handling an irate internal customer, he tried a new approach. Instead of delegating a specific tactic to Louise for handling the next interaction with the client (which was often his automatic type of response to employee mistakes in the past), he asked Louise if she was willing to explore some new tactics for negotiating deliverables with the client. And as they did, Louise gained greater insight about how her negative feelings about this client affected her performance. While Frank and she surfaced potential new tactics to handling an upcoming conversation with the client, he acknowledged that these tactics might feel uncomfortable for her to use at first but that he would support her through the situation. It was going to be a stretch, but with Frank's backing, Louise was willing to expand her repertoire for negotiating deliverables. This is a great illustration of combining the use of practices 1 and 2 (in this case, turning current work efforts into learning moments and raising employee self-awareness) before possibly moving on to practice 4 ("Teach skills to navigate the political terrain").

With the first two practices in place, you are well on your way to continually raising the capability of people to achieve higher levels of impact. You have the base from which to blend all five practices for your particular circumstances.

Your efforts to connect people with development partners (practice 3) becomes a natural complement to the first two practices. Since you've already done the foundational work of assessing your employees' skills and expanding the space for learning and doing (practice 1) and helping them become more self-aware (practice 2), you and they can feel confident that the independent learning taken from work with development partners will be a worthwhile use of everyone's time and effort. Practice 3 is especially helpful when your attention is needed elsewhere and the development partner can provide a level of guidance you may not have in your tool kit. Conversely, an employee with whom you have not provided support during key interactions (practice 2) may not be ready for working with development partners. Your employee may still be unaware of the negative impression he makes when he complains incessantly, for instance. You don't want to pawn that weakness onto a development partner who has volunteered to help you out by teaching time management skills. Imagine how the willing development partner Kara would feel if your employee Brandon won't stop griping to her about why her suggestions won't work.

Teaching skills to help navigate organization politics (practice 4) will make an important difference for employees whose work is highly interdependent with others', especially those outside the department. If you have few such employees (for example, if your employees interact mostly with you or work independently, as in a record-keeping or analytics department), you may not need to tap this practice very often. On the other hand, if you manage a function that serves internal or external customers (as, for instance, company strategy or program build- ers or key customer account reps do), it's possible you will be tapping in to practice 4 on a daily basis until your employees get so good at the political dynamics that they are teaching you a thing or two. If you're teaching politics to employees who will need to use them regularly, the self-awareness and self-man- agement skills honed through practice 2 are must-haves! Oth- erwise, during a sensitive political situation, they could make interpersonal faux pas and not even realize it. Also consider how helpful a development partner's perspective (practice 3) can be in understanding the political terrain.

Practice 5 ("Shape your environment to drive development") extends your daily use of the other practices by embedding the developmental focus into the work environment. Practice 1 is a ready foundation for your understanding of what needs to be emphasized in shaping an environment to drive develop- ment and for creating abundance. As for practice 5's other major component, managing the interface with the organiza- tion, your timing and effort level depend on your situation. You may need to manage the interface between your efforts and the rest of the organization early on (say, if the environment is not development-friendly and obstacles arise). Or you may be able to quietly and independently develop your prototype and portfolio of development tactics without involving people outside your department. In all cases, you'll need to monitor the interface to protect the gains you and your people are making and to use available companywide training and talent management tools to your department's best advantage.

By now you see how the patterns of an EDM practice are shaped by the department's circumstances and the needs of each individual employee. At this point, some readers may feel like they have just been through a high school class on combinations and permeations, but there is no need for worry. Once you are adept at using the practices, the way you combine them for the need at hand will come to you more naturally.

Summoning Up Resilience in the Face of Challenges

This is not the e-mail we want to receive from a reader twelve months down the road: "Dear Wendy and Jeannie, I worked hard at learning the five EDM practices from the book, but they are impossible to apply in my company. Too much stuff gets in the way. May I please have a refund?"

Just as you would help your employees understand that obstacles are out there, lurking around every bend, anticipate that you, too, will come upon challenges as you put your exceptional development practices into high gear. EDMs tell us that the most obvious challenges come from their direct role accountabilities—the pressure from their organizations to deliver results now, implying that the development of employees needs to be put off. Business urgencies such as the need to increase quarterly performance, address uncooperative stakeholders, and handle budget cuts can all seemingly undermine development efforts.

Sometimes the challenge may take the form of a reluctant employee. Encountering a "leave me alone and let me do my work" attitude can be dismaying, especially if the manager either needs the employee to perform at a higher level or sees that a great opportunity for growth is at hand. Then there are the challenges of a more immediate nature: managers' own habits that block their accomplishment of development results. They may get stuck "waiting for the right time" or allow themselves to be stymied by "too few resources." This litany of challenges from a multitude of sources can feel overwhelming.

The EDMs we spoke with experienced all of the aforementioned challenges yet were able to push through to the other side. In part, that's what has made them EDMs: they stared down the challenges over and over again. The key for most of them? Resilience. Finding a positive way to adapt to the pressures around them allowed the EDMs to put their exceptional development practices into action. Their resilience wasn't a matter of sheer determination driven by their strong values—although values provided a firm foundation for forward movement. They applied a handful of tactics that helped them punch through the walls. Take a look at these "Good Ideas" for inspiration.

Good Ideas . . .
For Summoning Up Resilience
in the Face of Challenges

Tapping into your values and reminding yourself of what motivates you to put your EDM practices into action is a great starting place. Here are a handful of familiar actions and representative examples you can use to knock down the wall of resistance.

» Keep your focus on the anticipated outcome, not specific tactics.

Think: *"I want to increase this staff members' financial know-how"* rather than *"I should send her to the university program on financial acumen."*

» If your first and second attempts don't work, keep going by trying a new tactic.

» If delegating stretch duties to an employee didn't get him to increase his strategic thinking, have him explore strategy online or in board games and report how these apply to your business operation.

» When there's no time to do it all, do less rather than put it all off.

» Can't afford a staff member's time off the job to have her manage a task force? Provide her with a couple of team members to manage a project that's within her current set of duties. Here's another solution: if there's no time to do it all, rather than put it off, do some now and some later. (Parcel the effort into chunks over a longer period of time.)

» Work through conflicts and disagreements rather than avoid unpleasant interactions.

» If your manager doesn't see the value of investing in a certain individual, spend the time to remind him or her of your EDM goals, make your case, and negotiate a practical outcome.

Surmounting challenges such as deadline imperatives, uncooperative stakeholders, budget cuts, and complaints from clients is really tough work. You're bound to feel overwhelmed, time-stressed, and perhaps even lonely (as in "Doesn't anyone out there get what I am trying to accomplish here?"). Mark, a strong businessman in the trucking industry, was a softie when it came to caring for his people. Management bombarded him with big concerns about grabbing larger market share and asked him to hold off on training programs. He resolved this tension by remembering his self-selected main priority as a manager: provide ongoing development for his people. He would simply have to figure out how to make it happen despite the "noise" from the organization. Like the managers mentioned in Chapter 5, Mark took his actions below the radar and simply didn't announce he was providing rotational assignments to continue employee development.

On one occasion. the very act of being resilient when faced with a pressure increased EDM Paula's capacity and ideas for facing challenges the next time. An administrator at a large non-profit, she told us, "I have adapted a new mantra: be aware of short-term pain for long-term gain." That mantra, she told us, gets her over humps of expecting perfection and instant results from her developing employees' efforts. Being part of a community-based organization with limited funds for training, she actually feels it is her duty to develop employees and broaden their skill sets. After facing a shortage of funds to bring in trainers she needed, she got a few external volunteers willing to help. From that point on, Paula was on fire, figuring out all kinds of ways to get her people developed—including getting them invited into the training centers of their corporate sponsors. The next time you're faced with a roadblock that tries to stop your forward movement, imagine how overcoming the challenge will increase both your confidence and insight for the next round of challenge.

3. Savor the Rewards

Have you ever taken a long-distance trip for business and been were amazed by what unfolded before you when you arrived? You went with one intention (get the presentation delivered), not realizing the impact that seeing the unique architecture, people interactions, and appealing shops would have on your thoughts, feelings, and conversations with your travel colleagues. You were transported in more ways than one, and maybe even phoned home to share your excitement about it. A similar phenomenon occurs when you put exceptional development practices into action. Almost always, the original intention is about helping to develop depth and breadth in your employees. The ultimate impact is far more substantial. There are additional layers of benefits (sometimes unforeseen) for employees, positive talent perks for companies, and outstanding professional and personal rewards for you as well. Let's take a closer look.

Rewards for Employees

When asked about his most memorable development experiences with an exceptional manager, Kal, an exceptional developing employee (EDE), told us, "He taught me lessons about handling myself in tricky interactions that have stuck with me for years. Guess I need to go back and tell him how important he was in my career." Even more than the enhancement of specific capabilities needed in current and near-term roles, EDMs provide what many employees are passionately looking for: the opportunity to significantly stretch and develop. They want that thrill as part of their everyday work experience, and you can provide it through daily development. For willing employees, your efforts can:

+ Expand their approaches to learning—understanding better the value of hands-on learning, the benefit of debriefs, and knowing that there are many (previously) hidden opportunities for learning every day

+ Spur them to find new ways to contribute, encouraging them to take on different roles that were not necessarily the next logical extension of their current job

+ Increase their reputation as the "go-to" person who's willing to stretch and enjoys it

+ Boost their careers through increasing their abilities to take on more complex tasks independently and master new skills, opening up the possibilities for bonuses or bigger jobs

+ Help them sail through complex situations with ease while others stumble

The employees we have managed in this way were great contributors when we worked together and have now become permanent members of our networks. Though they have moved away and had many careers changes, we always keep in touch. A handwritten note Wendy recently received underscores what one EDE felt was so important in her own development: "I can't express enough my appreciation for the time you've spent coaching me, for the candid feedback, for giving me the feeling of not being judged, and for the 'light bulbs' you lit."

Some may even translate their self-awareness and confidence into personal growth that helps their relationships at home and their effectiveness in nonwork environments. One of Jeannie's EDEs told her, "I am a force to be reckoned with on the school board because of the lessons you taught me. I actually find myself saying 'what would Jeannie do?' when I meet messy situations." Knowing the kind of impact we make with our staff and protégés are among our most treasured career moments.

Rewards for the Organization

Rewards abound at the organizational level as well. As the EDMs' roles shift from mostly performance managers to largely developers, their shops become "learning centers" that others know about. They attract people interested in developing and turning in great results. These teams become the places to be. EDMs, because they have given considerable attention to employees' skill levels, also provide accurate input regarding the company's talent management process. One HR director in a client organization told us, "I am not sure how she does it, but Char provides the most incredible detail about her employees' development needs. I really appreciate the amazing effort she has put into building their skills. Wish we could clone her." And it doesn't stop there. EDMs' efforts pay other types of dividends companies crave: attracting the best new recruits, readying employees for more complex roles, accelerating the development of high potentials more adeptly than others, and retaining high-producing employees even in the best of economic times.

You may recall a client organization we mentioned in the Introduction, an insurance company whose managers really wanted to provide more development for its employees but didn't know how. This company had dedicated tremendous effort to its talent management processes and, based on candid feedback from managers, decided it needed to invest even more to have the desired impact. The company provided tailor-made development for all its managers that was specifically geared to raising the bar on their development capabilities. Now how impressive is that?

Rewards for You

That brings us to the last layer of rewards: those that you as an EDM personally reap from your efforts. "Once I figured out that developing people was my main job, I had a whole new perspective on my career. I absolutely love doing this; I look forward to coming into work every day." This EDM, unknown to us before the research, even followed up with us after that interview, hungry to learn more about developing his people. Many EDMs tell us that perfecting their exceptional development practices as they make talent their business has yielded incredible personal rewards, far beyond what they originally imagined.

It's every manager's dream to have a terrific high-performing team that can work independently. That means that there will be fewer mistakes for you to clean up, greater autonomy for employees to make decisions independently, more time to focus on the big picture, and more opportunities to take on bigger and increasingly interesting projects. One manager who worked this way for more than twenty years told us, "It makes my job easier when people have confidence and skills to solve problems themselves. If people have this foundation, they can come in with 'here's the situation; here's how I think about it; this is what I will do.'"

Your reputation as an EDM will precede you. Good companies notice when managers find solutions to their problems or blaze new trails that take the whole organization forward. The people you develop and who move up and across the organization to achieve great things will be your primary messengers. As one EDM told us, "Your people promote you when you develop them." You'll develop a reputation for being a great manager, and it's likely you'll be promoted and retained because of it. And if you're not—either because economic conditions lead to wide-scale layoffs or because your organization somehow doesn't notice or value your contribution—you will have a skill that is both portable and sought-after. Every dynamic organization needs "people development" or "talent development" skills. You'll have a portfolio of experiences to bring to each new challenge, and we're willing to bet you'll find a new job more quickly than if you didn't have demonstrable people development skills.

The crowning jewel is often the gratification felt by others you affect—your legacy. When you provide your brand of managing people, each week brings added satisfaction that goes beyond productivity. EDMs we interviewed overwhelmingly talked about the deeply personal payback of growing others. Consider this: after you have mastered your functional skills, developing others may be the largest contribution you make in your work life. You will be in the enviable position to inspire your employees to much greater contributions with lessons that are remembered for their entire careers. Clayton Christensen, a renowned leadership expert, hopes that managers will latch onto this power early in their careers. He writes, "More and more MBA students come to school thinking that a career in business means buying, selling, and investing in companies. That's unfortunate. Doing deals doesn't yield the deep rewards that come from building up people."[9]

What are you waiting for? EDMs everywhere are already savoring these rewards. Most people wait until the end of their career to create their legacy, but you can start right now, making small deposits. The five proven practices for making talent your business will help transform your employees, your team's performance, and most especially, you.

 ## Consider This
What We've Been Told

Once you have made your investment in putting your exceptional development practices into action, you can anticipate your own version of the types of rewards we have heard about from others.

We have used the insights of our EDMs all the way through this book. We close by sharing some of our favorite comments about the rewards they receive from making talent their business.

» "Utter satisfaction, knowing I have helped develop others. Though my job title has not changed, I have now made developing people my main job."

» "I have far fewer headaches, less cleanups, and more independent staff."

» "My cycle of developing staff never ends. The company always gives me more people to develop, and I am fine with that."

» "For a long time, the company had so many talent development programs but they didn't give me a role. After finally figuring out how to do development in my own shop, the attitude of my staff has totally transformed—they enjoy coming to work every day. . . . I feel really proud of that."

» "It puts me into an ongoing development mode of my own. I get so much from the exchanges with my employees."

» "My hands are freer to do strategy work now that my staff have grown in capabilities and are eager to help each other over the daily bumps."

» "The more I operate as a developmental manager, the more my stock has grown in our company. . . . It led to some really wonderful assignments."

» "I got my last promotion because my competitor with equal technical and business skills lacked the experience to really develop staff."

» "My heart sings each time I get a call or e-mail from a former employee asking for my advice on a life change or sharing some big news."

Key Points for Putting Exceptional Development Practices into Action

▸▸ Initiate the transformation of your role. Clarify your motivation for increasing your capabilities to make talent your business. It will help put gas in your tank for the journey ahead.

▸▸ Become adept at combining and sequencing the five practices to fit the needs of your employees, given your business context. Start with practice 1, "Make every day a development day," and practice 2, "Tap into the psychological side of development," to create a foundation for the other three practices.

▸▸ Join in the development: identify the skills you need to make to put your exceptional development practices into action.

▸▸ Resolve to be resilient in the face of challenges. No transformation is ever easy, and you'll need to address roadblocks that you encounter. Each time you do, you may find more confidence and ideas for addressing the next one.

▸▸ Get ready for the good stuff. Rewards abound. Know that while your department gets better results, employees will thrive on the opportunities and your company will reap competitive benefits. Best of all, your career will prosper, and you will feel more fulfilled at work as you experience the deep satisfaction of developing others.

Acknowledgments

CREATING THIS BOOK, LIKE EVERYTHING we talk about in the book, was a developmental process requiring lots of support and guidance from others. We reached out to a multitude of people: many colleagues who are top experts in their fields, exceptional development managers (EDMs) and exceptional development employees (EDEs) both known and unknown to us before our research, an amazing editorial/publishing team, and those closest to us, our cherished family and friends.

We had our earliest conversations about this book with our dear colleagues Ellen Glanz and Linda Rodman, who cheered us on throughout our literary journey. We tapped a wide array of colleagues to help us identify qualified candidates for the research study. We are so grateful to all of our generous referrers and particularly want to mention Christy Macchione, Lori Zukin, and Terry Rothermel. The willing managers and professionals we spoke with were so generous with their time and candid with their reflections. We started the project believing we knew much of what was significant about the manager's role in talent development. As it turns out, these anonymous research participants taught us plenty and served to inform and sharpen the book's five practices. Thank you. When we were finalizing our research, we were fortunate to have the scrutinizing feedback of Gerry Groe, Bill Maki, Steve Kortick, and Ellen Glanz.

The next phase of work brought us into the unfamiliar world of publishing. Diana Whitney, John Schuster, Bev Kaye, and Johanna Vondeling—what would we have done without your sage guidance and generous endorsements? You truly launched us. And for those who believe that writing a book means sitting at your computer and tapping out your ideas, as if writing a memo or e-mail, well, that is not how it goes. We had an amazing editorial and publishing team who probed, questioned, sparked, and at times dashed our (unrealistically) high spirits. They pushed us into unknown territory and new heights of writing, yet they had our backs the entire time. In other words, they were our EDMs! This group included the incomparable team from Berrett-Koehler: Jeevan Sivasubramaniam, Neal Maillet, Michael Crowley, Katie Sheehan, Richard Wilson, Dianne Platner, and Zoe Mackey, along with BK's cast of top-notch and highly responsive professionals, including Jon Peck of Dovetail Publishing Services. And then there was Katherine Armstrong, developmental editor par excellence, who gave us coaching like we were training for a marathon, an intense period of guiding all our moves. Thank you all.

Gratitude goes out to our cherished families and friends; your support buoyed us up and kept our sanity. Friends like Christy Macchione and Henry Bendinelli were both inspiring and soothing (depending on what was needed at the time—they always got it right). Wendy's supportive family is quite large, including siblings, in-laws, stepchildren, cousins, and dear friends (whom she considers family). Of greatest support, inspiration, and counsel were her three men, Andy, Aaron, and Jake. Jeannie's husband Jim, a fiction writer who died in November 2008, inspired her to follow his path as a professional writer and cheered her during the very beginning of the research for the book.

Notes

Introduction

1. Robert W. Eichinger, Cara Capretta Raymond, and Jim Peters, presentation at the 2005 Succession Management Conference, New York, October 17, 2005.
2. Samuel Taylor, "The Rime of the Ancient Mariner," 1797.
3. Hewitt Associates and Human Capital Institute, *The State of Talent Management: Today's Challenges, Tomorrow's Opportunities* (Washington, D.C.: Human Capital Institute, 2008).
4. Matthew Guthridge, Asmus B. Komm, and Emily Lawson, "Making Talent a Strategic Priority," *McKinsey Quarterly*, January 2008, https://www.mckinseyquarterly.com/ Making_talent_a_strategic_priority_2092
5. Calhoun W. Wick and Lu Stanton Leon, *The Learning Edge: How Smart Managers and Smart Companies Stay Ahead* (New York: McGraw-Hill, 1993), p. xii.

Chapter 1

1. Nelson Mandela, *Long Walk to Freedom* (New York: Little, Brown, 1994), pp. 379–449.
2. The original research from the Center for Creative Leadership (CCL), published by Morgan W. McCall Jr., Michael M. Lombardo, and Ann M. Morrison in *The Lessons of Experience: How Successful Executives Develop on the Job* (Lexington, Mass.: Lexington Press, 1988), found

that the majority of lessons came from experience on the job. Subsequently, CCL and others quantified the relative strength of each major source as 70 percent work experience, 20 percent from other people, and just 10 percent from coursework and reading.

3. Warren Bennis, *On Becoming a Leader* (New York: Basic Books, 2003), p. 34.

4. Elizabeth L. Axelrod, Helen Handfield-Jones, and Timothy A. Welsh, "The War for Talent, Part Two," *McKinsey Quarterly*, May 2001, http://www.mckinseyquarterly.com/The_war_for_talent_part_two_1035.

5. Diana Whitney, Amanda Trosten-Bloom, and Kae Rader, *Appreciative Leadership: Focus on What Works to Drive Winning Performance and Build a Thriving Organization* (New York: McGraw-Hill, 2010), p. 42.

6. Ram Charan, *What the CEO Wants You to Know: Using Business Acumen to Understand How Your Company Really Works* (New York: Random House, 2001), p. 103.

7. Lynda Gratton, *Glow: How You Can Radiate Energy, Innovation, and Success.* (San Francisco: Berrett-Koehler, 2009), p. 197.

Chapter 2

1. Daniel Goleman, *Emotional Intelligence: Why It Can Matter More Than IQ* (New York: Bantam Books, 1995).

2. Dennis Reina and Michelle Reina, *Rebuilding Trust in the Workplace: Seven Steps to Renew Confidence, Commitment, and Energy* (San Francisco: Berrett-Koehler, 2010), pp. 5–6.

3. Dennis Reina and Michelle Reina, *Trust and Betrayal in the Workplace: Building Effective Relationships in Your Organization*, 2nd ed. (San Francisco: Berrett-Koehler, 2006), p. 65.

4. Ibid., p. 17.

5. Ibid., p. 35.

6. Ibid., p. 59.

7. Warren Bennis, *On Becoming a Leader* (New York: Basic Books, 2003), p. 62.

8.   Daniel Pink, "RSA Animate—Drive: The Surprising Truth About What Motivates Us," Apr. 1, 2010, http://www.youtube.com/watch?v=u6XAPnuFjJc.

9.   James M. Kouzes and Barry Z. Posner, The Leadership Challenge, 4th ed. (San Francisco: Jossey-Bass, 2007).

10. Marilee Sprenger, *Becoming a "Wiz" at Brain-Based Teaching: How to Make Every Year Your Best Year* (Thousand Oaks, Calif.: Corwin Press, 2007).

Chapter 3

1.   Corporate Executive Board, *Creating Talent Champions, Vol. 1* (Arlington, Va.: Corporate Executive Board, 2008).

2.   Aleksandr Solzhenitsyn, *The First Circle*, trans. Thomas P. Whitney (London: Collins, 1968), p. 3.

3.   Dorothy Leonard and Walter Swap, "Deep Smarts," *Harvard Business Review*, September 2004, pp. 89–97.

Chapter 4

1.   John Kotter, *Power and Influence: Beyond Formal Authority* (New York: Free Press, 2008).

2.   Joel DeLuca, *Political Savvy: Systematic Approaches to Leadership Behind the Scenes*, 2nd ed. (Berwyn, Pa.: EBG Publications, 1999).

3.   Jeffrey Pfeffer, "Power Play," *Harvard Business Review*, July–August 2010, p. 87.

Chapter 5

1.   Morgan McCall, *High Flyers: Developing the Next Generation of Leaders* (Boston: Harvard Business School Press, 1998), p. 4.

2.   Martha Lagace, "Gerstner: Changing Culture at IBM," Harvard Business School Working Knowledge, December 9, 2002, http://hbswk.hbs.edu/archive/3209.html

3.   David Ulrich and Wendy Ulrich, *The Why of Work: How Great Leaders Build Abundant Organizations That Win* (New York: McGraw-Hill, 2010), p. 23.

4. Beverly Kaye and Sharon Jordan-Evans. *Love 'Em or Lose 'Em: Getting Good People to Stay* (San Francisco: Berrett-Koehler, 2005).

5. BlessingWhite, The State of Employee Engagement, 2008, blessingwhite.com/EEE_report.asp.

6. Michael M. Lombardo and Robert W. Eichinger, *The Leadership Machine: Architecture to Develop Leaders for Any Future* (Minneapolis, Minn.: Lominger Limited, 2002), p. 265.

Chapter 6

1. Racontours, "Building the Brooklyn Bridge," 2005, http://www.racontours.com/archive/building_the _brooklyn_bridge.php.

2. Gary Feuerstein, "Brooklyn Bridge Facts, History, and Information," 1998, http://www.endex.com/gf/buildings/ bbridge/bbridgefacts.htm.

3. Wikipedia, "Brooklyn Bridge," http://en.wikipedia.org/wiki/ Brooklyn_Bridge.

4. Feuerstein, "Brooklyn Bridge."

5. Lynne Morton, *Talent Management Value Imperatives: Strategies for Execution* (New York: Conference Board, 2005).

6. Bill Conaty and Ram Charan, *The Talent Masters: Why Smart Leaders Put People Before Numbers* (New York: Crown, 2010), p. 2.

7. Chip Heath and Dan Heath, *Made to Stick: Why Some Ideas Survive and Others Die* (New York: Random House, 2007).

8. Billy Kirk, "Does Light Travel in a Straight Line?" eHow, n.d., http://www.ehow.com/how-does_4569984_does-light -travel-straight-line.html.

9. Clayton Christensen, "How Will You Measure Your Life? Don't Reserve Your Best Business Thinking for Your Career," *Harvard Business Review*, July–August 2010, p. 48.

Index

About the Research

In our work with individual managers and companies to build leadership development capabilities, instill corporate cultures that support talent development, and teach managers how to make talent their business, we identified a significant gap between the sincere desire to develop people's potential and the stark reality that most organizations fall short of their people development goals. This gap was also highlighted in the research we cited in the Introduction. The net conclusion: there are managers in all kinds of organizations with all the right intentions but few of the right skills or tangible support mechanisms to develop staff fully. We embarked on research to better understand and then help close this gap. Our aim was to determine when and how managers make a significant impact on developing talent.

Over a period of a year, ending in October 2009, we conducted in-depth interviews with more than seventy-five people from well-known companies. We also tapped into smaller firms, reaching representatives from twenty-eight such companies in total. We spoke with both "exceptional development managers," who were identified as people who truly develop the capacity of their employees beyond day-to-day performance needs, and "exceptional developing employees" who search out and seize growth opportunities. Both groups of people we interviewed were prequalified on the basis of several criteria to ensure that they were exceptionally development-focused. Most of the study participants were unknown to us prior to the study and were not our current clients. The results of our research were distilled into the five practices for making talent your business that are covered in this book.

In conducting our interviews, we used an interview protocol with standardized questions, and we even standardized "probe" questions for supplemental inquiries. Unlike many anonymous online research questionnaires, this personal interaction allowed our participants to provide greater detail in areas they thought were most crucial, and we appreciated learning from them.

We used two primary forms of data analysis: content analysis of qualitative questions and statistical analysis of rated survey items. Themes from the open- ended interview questions, statistical analysis of the survey items, and a full discussion of the research are contained in the research report available at http://talentsavvymanager.com/Learning.html.

Partial List of Source Companies

Individuals we interviewed from these companies represented their own views, not necessarily the views of their employers.

Adidas	Genentech	L'Oréal
Axian	GlaxoSmithKline	Marriott
AXA	IBM	Merck
Blount	Intel	Microsoft
Booz Allen Hamilton	ID Experts	MGM Mirage
	JPMorgan Chase	NW Natural
Corning	Kaiser Permanente	Siemens
Devon Energy	Knowledge Learning	Wells Fargo
FINRA		
First Advantage	Kraft	Wyeth
GE Interlogix	Kronos	Xerox

Figures 1–8 provide an overview of the participant demographics for both exceptional development managers (EDMs) and exceptional developing employees (EDEs).

Demographics of Research Participants

Exceptional Development Managers

Figure 1 ■ Gender

Figure 2 ■ Years in Workforce

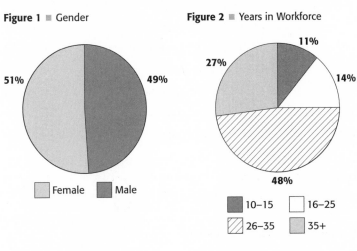

Figure 3 ■ Age

Figure 4 ■ Level

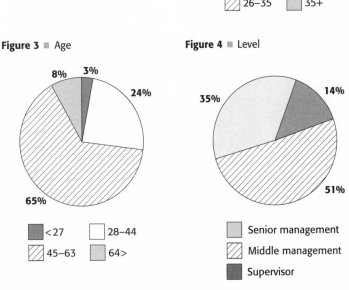

Exceptional Developing Employees

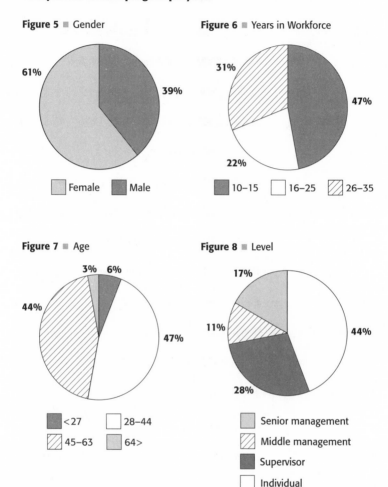

Figure 5 ■ Gender

61% / 39%

Female　Male

Figure 6 ■ Years in Workforce

31% / 47% / 22%

10–15　16–25　26–35

Figure 7 ■ Age

3%　6% / 44% / 47%

<27　28–44
45–63　64>

Figure 8 ■ Level

17% / 11% / 44% / 28%

Senior management
Middle management
Supervisor
Individual

Summarized Response Ratings: Practices Managers Use to Drive Development (Comparison Between Managers and Employees)

While much of the data we captured was qualitative through interviews, we did ask participants to respond to survey questions. One survey question asked about the extent to which managers used certain practices to drive development. Figure 9 shows the average responses, based on a scale of their reported frequency, from

Figure 9 ▪ EDM Development Practices and EDE Reports of Use

1. Provide air cover while staff learns	
2. Ask thoughtful questions	
3. Give clear feedback	
4. Manage for outcomes rather than activities	
5. Regular discussions about learning from work	
6. Remove organization obstacles	
7. Provide stretch assignments	
8. Target work assignments	
9. Identify what to learn	
10. Open doors to people resources	
11. Just-in-time links to books and training	
12. Encourage learning outside of organization	
13. Set up job shadow/ job share	

■ EDMs
☐ EDEs

1, almost never, to 6, almost always. The EDMs reported on their own use of these practices. EDEs rated the frequency of the use of these practices by their most outstanding developmental manager.

We are most grateful to our participants for their candor during these interviews and for their over-the-top enthusiasm about exceptional development practices. They provided the richness of material that made it possible to write this book. Without exception, these participants truly made talent their business.

About the Authors

Wendy Axelrod, Ph.D.

WENDY AXELROD'S ABIDING INTEREST in developing the "people side" of the organization to match and spur organization aspirations has been consistent for more than twenty-five years. Her spirited and results-driven approach to collaborating with line executives and human resource leaders has helped her clients bring about growth for their leaders, workforce, and businesses.

Wendy's own development of strategic focus, organizational development capabilities, and leadership development skills were cultivated through connections with a capable cadre of managers, colleagues, and employees, during her sixteen years with Sunoco. As an HR executive, she transformed the corporate university to distinctively advance the company's business objectives, led the talent management function to create a competitive leadership pipeline, and served as chief architect to ensure a highly successful multiyear culture transformation.

Wendy, along with Jeannie Coyle, is managing partner of Talent Savvy Manager, a consulting firm that helps managers and organizations drive substantial development of people to create real long-term winning performance. She has collaborated with management in dozens of organizations to develop their organization, leaders, and workforce. She has led efforts such as designing a robust and adaptive corporate university, bringing about cultural transformation to align organization practices with company goals, and assessing talent management systems and formulating long-term talent management strategies. She serves as a designer and facilitator of cutting-edge leadership development and as an executive coach. In her decade-long association with the Forum Corporation, as a facilitator and executive coach, she has been Forum's annual North American ResNet recipient of the Award for Excellence. Some of her clients have included Deloitte, Novo Nordisk, Shire, Duke Energy, American Family Insurance, Northrop Grumman, Vanguard, Occidental, Sanofi, and Merck. Her years of experience have settled squarely on helping managers and leaders become exceptional developers of others.

Wendy's volunteer leadership with professional associations and nonprofits has been wonderfully developmental for her as well and helped form a strong values orientation, which she brings to her entire life. A longtime board member and former president of the Philadelphia affiliate of the Human Resource People and Strategy organization, Wendy has been one of two individuals to receive the organization's Lifetime Achievement Award (relatively early in her career!). The "best practices" mentoring program she launched and leads has received wide attention. Wendy also supports the University of Pennsylvania's Wharton School Global Consulting Practicum as a member of the Devil's Advocate panel. She has served on several nonprofit boards and speaks at professional association meetings and conferences.

Her undergraduate degree was received from Drexel University, where she was awarded the M.M. Creese Scholarship and Award for Outstanding Senior Woman of the University. Wendy's graduate degrees, culminating with a doctorate in organization psychology, are from Colorado State University. She is licensed in many leadership development tools.

Wendy has two sons and three stepchildren and lives near Philadelphia with her husband, Andy.

Jeannie Coyle

FOR FOUR DECADES, TWO PERCEPTIONS have deeply informed Jeannie Coyle's passion and professional practice: first, that significant investment in people is the core of business success, and second, that people learn from experience on the job—with support from leaders who are in the perfect spot to support learning. With the rigor of research, Wendy and Jeannie have discovered how to bring these two ideas together in the five practices that enable managers to truly develop higher levels of capability among their staff and at the same time increase business results. They have joined forces to launch Talent Savvy Manager, a firm dedicated to the application of these practices.

During her early career, Jeannie earned her stripes in New York City's financial industry, first at Mutual of New York and then at American Express, where she honed her strategic HR craft through accelerated development on the job. Increasing responsibilities during her eleven years there propelled her through the leadership pipeline and kept her continually on the learning edge. She had the opportunity to amplify her experience as an apprentice to a premiere exceptional development manager. He taught her well how to discover the drivers for making the critical and highly focused changes in leadership, workforce, and organizational capabilities that lead to business growth.

All this learning paid off when Jeannie was promoted to senior vice-president of human resources at American Express and partnered with her boss, Lou Gerstner, to create an enduring talent management system for organically growing leaders for the longer term. Next, San Francisco beckoned, and her career continued at Bank of America. There she designed and implemented a global leadership development program as vice-president of leadership development and led a creative revamping of the job design and compensation system that transformed the work and rewards for the Systems and Operations Group.

Jeannie founded her first consulting company in 1986. Early on, she became a strategic partner of the Tom Peters Group, implementing an innovative program designed to create customer-responsive cultures. She has collaborated with many senior management executives to align the "people side" with business strategy execution through leadership coaching, design of leadership development systems, and tuning up organizational design and culture. She works across industries with clients such as 3M, Intel, Nike, Time Warner, S. C. Johnson, American Express, GE Capital, Pacific Gas and Electric, Pac Bell, the *New York Times*, CompuCom, Kaiser Permanente, and Wells Fargo, as well as many smaller fast-growing firms.

She has been a board member of HR People and Strategy (HRPS) for two terms and a member of the executive committee for seven years. She is currently on the board of the Pacific Northwest HR Strategic Forum. Jeannie regularly provides engaging keynote addresses on leadership, strategic HR, and coaching at client conferences. She has appeared as a presenter at HRPS, ASTD, and SHRM meetings and conferences.

Jeannie earned a bachelor of arts degree with honors at Saint Louis University. She teaches in the M.B.A. programs of Marylhurst University and Portland State University in Portland, Oregon, where she currently resides.

Wendy Axelrod   *Jeannie Coyle*

More information about Wendy and Jeannie and how to contact them can be found at their Web site

http://www.TalentSavvyManager.com.

Berrett–Koehler
Publishers

Berrett-Koehler is an independent publisher dedicated to an ambitious mission: *Creating a World That Works for All*.

We believe that to truly create a better world, action is needed at all levels—individual, organizational, and societal. At the individual level, our publications help people align their lives with their values and with their aspirations for a better world. At the organizational level, our publications promote progressive leadership and management practices, socially responsible approaches to business, and humane and effective organizations. At the societal level, our publications advance social and economic justice, shared prosperity, sustainability, and new solutions to national and global issues.

A major theme of our publications is "Opening Up New Space." Berrett-Koehler titles challenge conventional thinking, introduce new ideas, and foster positive change. Their common quest is changing the underlying beliefs, mindsets, institutions, and structures that keep generating the same cycles of problems, no matter who our leaders are or what improvement programs we adopt.

We strive to practice what we preach—to operate our publishing company in line with the ideas in our books. At the core of our approach is stewardship, which we define as a deep sense of responsibility to administer the company for the benefit of all of our "stakeholder" groups: authors, customers, employees, investors, service providers, and the communities and environment around us.

We are grateful to the thousands of readers, authors, and other friends of the company who consider themselves to be part of the "BK Community." We hope that you, too, will join us in our mission.

A BK Business Book

This book is part of our BK Business series. BK Business titles pioneer new and progressive leadership and management practices in all types of public, private, and nonprofit organizations. They promote socially responsible approaches to business, innovative organizational change methods, and more humane and effective organizations.

Berrett–Koehler
Publishers

A community dedicated to creating
a world that works for all

Visit Our Website: www.bkconnection.com

Read book excerpts, see author videos and Internet movies, read
our authors' blogs, join discussion groups, download book apps, find
out about the BK Affiliate Network, browse subject-area libraries of
books, get special discounts, and more!

Subscribe to Our Free E-Newsletter, the *BK Communiqué*

Be the first to hear about new publications, special discount offers,
exclusive articles, news about bestsellers, and more! Get on the list
for our free e-newsletter by going to **www.bkconnection.com**.

Get Quantity Discounts

Berrett-Koehler books are available at quantity discounts for orders
of ten or more copies. Please call us toll-free at (800) 929-2929 or
email us at bkp.orders@aidcvt.com.

Join the BK Community

BKcommunity.com is a virtual meeting place where people from
around the world can engage with kindred spirits to create a world
that works for all. **BKcommunity.com** members may create their own
profiles, blog, start and participate in forums and discussion groups,
post photos and videos, answer surveys, announce and register for
upcoming events, and chat with others online in real time. Please join
the conversation!

Mixed Sources
Product group from well-managed
forests and recycled wood or fiber
www.fsc.org Cert no. SW-COC-003925
© 1996 Forest Stewardship Council
FSC